God's Wonderful Love

A Catholic Prayer Book of Affirmation, Gratitude, and Worship.

Compiled by Deena Philip

Copyright © 2026 DEENA PHILIP
All rights reserved

Title: God's Wonderful Love
ISBN: 978-1-7638433-9-4
Author: Deena Philip
Category: Non-fiction, Religious Prayer Book
Cover design by: Deena Philip

Disclaimer
This prayer book is intended for personal devotion and encouragement in faith. The prayers contained within are offered as a companion for reflection, meditation, and a prayerful connection with God. They are not a substitute for the teachings of the Holy Catholic Church, the guidance of ordained clergy, or the Sacraments.
Readers are encouraged to use this book alongside Sacred Scripture, the Catechism of the Catholic Church, and the guidance of their parish community. This book is offered for spiritual encouragement only and does not replace professional, pastoral, medical, or legal guidance.

All inquiries should be made to the publisher / author at the address provided below.
Supported By Cheer Publishing, Australia
www.cheerproductions.com.au
Author's email:
reach2rosebutterfly@gmail.com
team4deen@gmail.com

About This Book

This book contains 7 Prayers of Gratitude, which you may say each day of the week or as your heart guides you.

Each month features a special affirmation and a prayer for every day, helping you to grow in faith, hope, and love as you walk with God.

At the end of the book, you will find a **Daily Affirmation**, which you may choose to recite each day.

Additional prayers and devotions included are:

- Thanksgiving Prayer at Year's end
- New Year Blessings
- Prayer for Courage
- Daily Affirmation

- Prayer for the Gifts of the Holy Spirit
- Prayer for the Fruits of the Holy Spirit
- Prayer before Work
- Prayer to Holy Family
- Infant Jesus Novena
- Chaplet of Divine Mercy with 3'o clock prayer.
- Apostles' Creed
- The Rosary, complete with the Litany to the Blessed Virgin Mary and the Saints
- Haily Holy Queen

Remember to pray every day.

Contents

Prayer of Gratitude for Daily Blessings 7

Prayer of Gratitude for Life's Abundance 8

Prayer of Gratitude for Guidance and
Relationships 10

Prayer of Gratitude for Strength, Courage, and
Purpose 12

Prayer of Gratitude for Family, Peace, and
Blessings 14

Prayer of Gratitude for Health, Vitality,
and Joy 16

Prayer of Gratitude for Life's Journey 18

New Year Blessing 20

JANUARY 21

FEBRUARY 43

MARCH 64

APRIL 88

MAY 109

JUNE 128

JULY 151

AUGUST 174

SEPTEMBER 196

OCTOBER 219

NOVEMBER 237

DECEMBER	258
A Thanksgiving Prayer at Year's End	282
Daily Affirmation — Health, Wealth, Love, and Success	283
Prayer for Courage	283
Prayer for the Gifts of the Holy Spirit	284
Prayer for the Fruits of the Holy Spirit	285
Prayer Before Work	286
Infant Jesus of Prague Novena Prayer	288
Prayer to the Holy Family	289
Chaplet of Divine Mercy	291
The Apostles' Creed	293
The Lord's Prayer	294
Rosary: How to Pray the Rosary	295
Joyful Mysteries — Monday & Saturday	296
Sorrowful Mysteries — Tuesday & Friday	298
Glorious Mysteries — Wednesday & Sunday	301
Luminous Mysteries — Thursday	304
Hail Holy Queen	306
Litany of the Blessed Virgin Mary (Litany of Loreto)	308
Saints	312
Find Prayer:	315

1

Prayer of Gratitude for Daily Blessings

Heavenly Father,
I thank You for the gift of life and all the blessings You have given me.
Thank You for my health, my family, my friends, and the love that surrounds me.
Thank You for the beauty of creation, the wonders of nature, and the joy of each new day.
Thank You for the talents, skills, and gifts You have placed within me.
Thank You for fun, laughter, and the opportunities to grow, learn, and share Your love.
Help me to use all these blessings wisely, to glorify You in all I do,
and to always walk with a heart full of gratitude.
Amen.

2

Prayer of Gratitude for Life's Abundance

Heavenly Father,
I thank You with all my heart for the abundance of happiness in my life.
Thank You for the precious moments of family time, the love and laughter we share. Thank You for the joys of travelling and discovering the beauty of Your creation around the world.
Thank You for the success in my work and the opportunities to grow and use my talents.
Thank You for the delicious food that nourishes me and the companionship of friends who enrich my days.
Thank You for every gift, seen and unseen, that fills my life with joy, hope, and peace.
Help me to always recognize Your hand

Prayer of Gratitude for Life's Abundance

in all things, to share my blessings with others, and to live each day with a grateful and loving heart.
Amen.

3

Prayer of Gratitude for Guidance and Relationships

Heavenly Father,
I thank You for the gift of the Holy Spirit, who fills my heart with wisdom, guidance, and peace.
Thank You for helping me make wise decisions in my life and for the clarity to navigate challenges.
Thank You for the patience, understanding, and kindness You cultivate in me, enabling me to deal with people and nurture healthy relationships.
Thank You for the sympathy and compassion You place in my heart, for good behaviour, and for the opportunities to show love and respect to others.
Thank You for moments when I feel

Prayer of Gratitude for Guidance and Relationships

understood, accepted, and celebrated for who I am.

May I continue to walk in Your Spirit, reflecting Your love, patience, and joy to everyone around me.

Amen.

4

Prayer of Gratitude for Strength, Courage, and Purpose

Heavenly Father,
I thank You for the strength and courage You give me each day to face challenges with ease and confidence.
Thank You for helping me complete my tasks on time, manage my responsibilities wisely, and use my time effectively.
Thank You for the physical and mental energy You provide, for perseverance in overcoming obstacles, and for the courage to stand up for what I believe.
Thank You for guiding me to share my ideas freely without fear of judgment, to live authentically, and to follow the path You have planned for me and my family.
Thank You for the clarity, focus, and

Prayer of Gratitude for Strength, Courage, and Purpose

determination that allow me to fulfill my purpose according to Your will.
I will continue to walk faithfully in Your guidance, reflecting Your strength, courage, and love in all that I do.
Amen.

5

Prayer of Gratitude for Family, Peace, and Blessings

Heavenly Father,
Thank You for the peace You bring into
our lives and for the wonderful ways
You work in each member of my family.
For my loving partner and my
wonderful children.
Thank You for keeping them healthy,
joyful, and at peace, and for making
their lives beautiful.
Thank You for letting them be seen,
accepted, and celebrated among their
friends, and for nurturing their skills
and talents so they flourish beautifully.
Thank You for helping us grow each day
in care, love, and understanding.
Thank You for the safety You provide,
for our peaceful and beautiful home, for
all the facilities, comfort, and space we

Prayer of Gratitude for Family, Peace, and Blessings

enjoy. Thank You for the greater blessings You are planning for us, and for guiding our hearts to embrace them with gratitude and faith.

Amen.

6

Prayer of Gratitude for Health, Vitality, and Joy

Heavenly Father,
Thank You for the gift of my body and health, for the strength and energy You give me each day.
Thank You for my appearance, my hair, my skin, and my body that is strong, radiant, and full of life.
Thank You for keeping me youthful in spirit, joyful in heart, and vibrant in energy.
Thank You for the beauty You have placed in me, for the confidence, radiance, and positivity that shine through.
Thank You for my playful, funny, and joyful nature, and for the laughter and light I can share with others.
Thank You for all the ways You help me

Prayer of Gratitude for Health, Vitality, and Joy

flourish, succeed, and grow in every aspect of my life.
Amen.

7

Prayer of Gratitude for Life's Journey

Heavenly Father, Jesus and Holy Spirit, thank You for all the things that have happened today, for the people You placed in my life, and for every experience I have lived.

Thank You for all that I accomplished and even for what I could not do. My successes and my failures are Your blessings, and I value and thank You for them.

It has helped me to be what I am today, and You have done it so beautifully, and I thank You for that. I believe and trust in Your plans.

Thank You for each member of my family, my teachers, my guardians, my friends, my colleagues, and for the guardian angels You keep beside me

Prayer of Gratitude for Life's Journey

always.
Thank You for shaping my yesterday,
my today, and my tomorrow.
Thank You, Father. Thank You, Jesus.
Thank You, Holy Spirit.
Amen.

New Year Blessing

I begin this year in God's light and protection.

Prayer

O God of new beginnings,
bless this year that lies before me.
Fill my days with Your peace,
my mind with Your wisdom,
and my heart with Your love.

Guide my steps, protect my family,
and strengthen my faith in every moment.

May this year draw me closer to You
in hope, trust, and joy.
Amen.

JANUARY

Month of New Beginnings

Affirmation for the Month:

This January, I embrace new beginnings in God's love. I am guided by His mercy, strengthened by His Spirit, and surrounded by His protection.

Day 1 — To God Our Father

God, my loving Father, You watch over me. I rest in Your care, trusting Your mercy and love to surround me.

Prayer

Watch, O Lord, with those who wake, or watch, or weep, and give Your angels charge over those who sleep.
Tend to Your sick ones, O Lord Christ; rest Your weary ones; bless Your dying ones; soothe Your suffering ones; pity Your afflicted ones; shield Your joyous ones; and all for Your love's sake. Amen.

— St. Augustine's Evening Prayer

Day 2 — To the Blessed Virgin Mary, Mother of God

Holy Mother Mary, you are my gentle guide. Guide me, hold me close, and lead me safely to your Son.

JANUARY

Prayer

Remember, O most gracious Virgin Mary, that never was it known that anyone who fled to your protection, implored your help, or sought your intercession, was left unaided. Inspired with this confidence, I fly to you, O Virgin of virgins, my Mother. To you I come, before you I stand, sinful and sorrowful. O Mother of the Word Incarnate, despise not my petitions, but in your mercy hear and answer me. Amen.

— *The Memorare (Traditional Marian Prayer)*

Day 3 — To the Holy Spirit, Comforter and Guide

Holy Spirit, my light and guide. Fill my heart with peace, my mind with clarity, and my soul with Your fire.

Prayer

Come, Holy Spirit, fill the hearts of Your faithful and enkindle in them the fire of Your love. Send forth Your Spirit, and they shall be created, and You shall renew the face of the earth. Amen.

— *"Veni Sancte Spiritus"*

Day 4 — To My Guardian Angel, Heavenly Protector

God's angels watch over me with love. I am never alone. My guardian angel is beside me, keeping me safe and guiding me.

Prayer

Angel of God, my guardian dear, to whom His love commits me here, ever be at my side, to light and guard, to rule and guide. Amen.

— *Traditional Guardian Angel Prayer*

JANUARY

Day 5 — To the Holy Family

Jesus, Mary, and Joseph, bless my family. Fill our hearts with love, our home with peace, and our lives with faith.

Prayer

Jesus, Mary, and Joseph, I give You my heart, my soul, my home, and my family. Bless us, guide us, and protect us always. Amen.

— *Prayer to the Holy Family*

Day 6 — Feast of the Epiphany

Lord, reveal Your light to me and all people. May I follow Your guidance and share Your love in everything I do.

Prayer

O Lord, You appeared to the nations as the true light. Grant that Your guidance may lead us to You with joyful hearts. Amen.— *Traditional Epiphany Prayer*

Day 7 — To Divine Mercy

Jesus, I trust in Your mercy.
Wash over me with Your love, forgive my sins, and guide my steps.

Prayer

Eternal God, in whom mercy is endless and the treasury of compassion inexhaustible, look kindly upon us and increase Your mercy in us, that in difficult moments we might not despair nor become despondent, but with great confidence submit ourselves to Your holy will, which is Love and Mercy itself. Amen.

— *Divine Mercy Prayer*

Day 8 — To the Sacred Heart of Jesus

Jesus, Your heart is my refuge.
Let Your love and mercy fill me and guide me in all I do.

Prayer

O Sacred Heart of Jesus, filled with infinite love and mercy, receive my heart. Purify it from all sin, and fill it with Your peace.
Amen.

— *From the Devotion to the Sacred Heart of Jesus*

Day 9 — To Saint Joseph, Protector of Families

Saint Joseph, guide and protect my family. Keep us safe and strong in faith, hope, and love.

Prayer

O Saint Joseph, guardian of the Redeemer, and devoted spouse of the Blessed Virgin Mary, protect us and guide us in our daily lives. Amen.

— *Traditional Prayer to Saint Joseph*

Day 10 — To the Blessed Virgin Mary, Comforter

Holy Mother Mary, I seek your care. Wrap me in your mantle of love and bring me comfort and hope.

Prayer

Mother Mary, hold me close under your mantle of love. When I feel worried or afraid, remind me that your Son watches over me always.
Amen.

— *Traditional Night Prayer to Mary*

Day 11 — To Saint Agnes, Pure and Faithful

Saint Agnes, model of purity and courage. Help me remain faithful to God in all I do and guard my heart with love and devotion.

Prayer

O Saint Agnes, you remained steadfast

in faith despite trials.

Pray for me, that I may remain pure in heart and strong in trust in God.

Amen.

— *Traditional Prayer to Saint Agnes*

Day 12 — To the Guardian Angel

God's angels watch over me with love. I am never alone. My guardian angel is beside me, keeping me safe and guiding me.

Prayer

Angel of God, my guardian dear, to whom His love commits me here, ever guide, protect, and inspire me in my journey of faith.

Amen.

— *Traditional Guardian Angel Prayer*

Day 13 — To Mother Mary, Star of the Sea

Mother Mary, guide me through life's storms. Lead me to Your Son and fill my heart with hope.

Prayer

O Mary, Star of the Sea, guide me through life's difficulties. Intercede for me with Your Son and protect me with Your love.
Amen.

— *Traditional Marian Devotion*

Day 14 — To Jesus, Light of the World

Jesus, shine Your light in my heart. Help me follow Your truth and reflect Your love.

Prayer

O Jesus, Light of the World, enlighten my mind and heart. Lead me in Your ways and strengthen my faith in You. Amen.

— *Inspired by John 8:12*

Day 15 — To the Holy Spirit, Source of Wisdom

Holy Spirit, fill me with understanding and strength. Guide my thoughts, decisions, and actions.

Prayer

Come, Holy Spirit, grant me wisdom, understanding, counsel, fortitude, knowledge, piety, and fear of the Lord. Help me follow God's will in all I do. Amen.

— *Traditional Gifts of the Holy Spirit Prayer*

Day 16 — To Saint Blaise, Protector of Health

Saint Blaise, guardian of health and faith. Watch over me, protect me from illness, and help me trust in God's healing grace.

Prayer

O Saint Blaise, holy intercessor and healer, shield me from all sickness and danger. Grant me health in body and spirit, and strengthen my faith in God's loving care.
Amen.

— *Traditional Prayer to Saint Blaise*

Day 17 — To Saint Francis de Sales, Patron of Gentle Hearts

Saint Francis, teach me gentleness and patience. Help me live each day with kindness, calmness, and trust in God's mercy.

Prayer

O Saint Francis de Sales, gentle and wise teacher of God's love, intercede for me that I may grow in patience, gentleness, and charity in all my actions. Amen.

— *Traditional Prayer to Saint Francis de Sales*

Day 18 — To Mother Mary, Comforter of Souls

Holy Mother Mary, guide me in faith. Bring peace to my heart and intercede for me with your Son.

Prayer

O Blessed Mother, comforter of souls, guide me in faith and protect me in all my ways.
May I always feel your loving presence. Amen.

— *Traditional Marian Prayer*

Day 19 — To Jesus, Divine Physician

Jesus, healer of all wounds. Restore my soul, renew my hope, and grant me strength to follow Your ways.

Prayer

O Divine Physician, heal the brokenness in my heart, mind, and body. Grant me courage, patience, and peace in all circumstances.
Amen.

— Inspired by Catholic Healing Devotions

Day 20 — To the Holy Spirit, Consoler of Hearts

Holy Spirit, bring comfort and understanding. Guide my decisions, inspire my prayers, and fill me with faith and peace.

Prayer

Come, Holy Spirit,
give me wisdom, understanding,

counsel, fortitude, knowledge, piety, and fear of the Lord. Let Your gifts guide me in all I do. Amen.

— Traditional Gifts of the Holy Spirit Prayer

Day 21 — To Saint Joseph, Terror of Demons

Saint Joseph, strong protector. Defend me from evil, protect my home, and guide me in faith.

Prayer

O Saint Joseph, Terror of Demons, stand between me and all spiritual harm. Guide my steps and lead me to safety in God's love. Amen.

— Traditional Prayer to Saint Joseph

Day 22 — To Mother Mary, Queen of Angels

Holy Mother Mary, watch over me.
Lead me with your angels' guidance and draw me closer to Your Son.

Prayer

Hail Mary, full of grace,
the Lord is with thee;
blessed art thou among women,
and blessed is the fruit of thy womb,
Jesus.
Holy Mary, Mother of God,
pray for us sinners, now and at the hour of our death.
Amen.

— *Traditional Hail Mary*

Day 23 — To Jesus, Bread of Life

Jesus, You sustain me. Feed my soul with Your Word, guide my heart with Your love, and strengthen my faith.

Prayer

O Jesus, Bread of Life,
nourish my soul and grant me
perseverance in Your love.
Help me trust You in all things and
grow in holiness.
Amen.

— *Inspired by John 6:35*

Day 24 — To Saint Valentine, Intercessor for Love

Saint Valentine, pray for my heart.
Teach me to love sincerely, forgive
freely, and live with joy in God's love.

Prayer

O Saint Valentine, obtain for me the
grace to love as God commands.
Strengthen my heart, guide my actions,
and protect those I hold dear. Amen.

— *Traditional Prayer to Saint Valentine*

Day 25 — Prayer for Serenity and Peace

Lord, grant me serenity, courage, and wisdom. Help me accept what I cannot change, act on what I can, and trust in You always.

Prayer

God, grant me the serenity
to accept the things I cannot change,
courage to change the things I can,
and wisdom to know the difference.
Living one day at a time, enjoying one moment at a time. Amen.

— *Traditional Serenity Prayer*

Day 26 — To Mother Mary, Help of Christians

Holy Mother Mary, aid me in faith and devotion. Guide me through trials and intercede for me with Your Son.

Prayer

O Mary, Help of Christians, protect me, guide me, and lead me always to Jesus. Strengthen my faith and trust in God's mercy.
Amen.

— *Traditional Marian Devotion*

Day 27 — To the Holy Spirit, Advocate and Guide

Holy Spirit, fill me with Your presence. Inspire my words, strengthen my faith, and enlighten my mind.

Prayer

Come, Holy Spirit, be my guide, my strength, and my comfort. Teach me to live in Your love and share Your gifts with others.
Amen.

— *Inspired by "Veni Sancte Spiritus"*

Day 28 — To Jesus, Prince of Peace
Jesus, bring peace to my heart.

Calm my worries, guide my thoughts, and help me live in love and patience.

Prayer

O Jesus, Prince of Peace,
fill my heart with Your calm and serenity.
Let Your peace reign in my soul and guide all my actions.
Amen.

— Traditional Devotion to Jesus, Prince of Peace

Day 29 — To Saint George, Defender of Faith

Saint George, protector and courageous warrior. Defend me from evil,
strengthen my faith, and inspire me to act with courage.

Prayer

O Saint George, valiant defender of Christ, help me remain strong in faith, resist evil, and live with courage, hope, and trust in God.
Amen.

— Traditional Prayer to Saint George

Day 30 — To the Sacred Heart of Jesus

Jesus, Your love is my refuge.
Fill my heart with mercy, peace, and trust in Your infinite care.

Prayer

O Sacred Heart of Jesus,
I place all my trust in You.
Guide me, comfort me, and lead me to holiness.
Amen.

— Sacred Heart Prayer Inspired

Day 31 — To Divine Mercy

Jesus, I trust in Your mercy and love. Help me begin each new day in faith, hope, and devotion.

Prayer

O Blood and Water, which gushed forth
from the Heart of Jesus
as a fount of mercy for us,
I trust in You.
Amen.

— Divine Mercy Prayer

FEBRUARY

Month of the Holy Family and the Flame of Love.

Affirmation for the Month:

In this month of love and devotion, I seek the peace of the Holy Family and the warmth of Christ's heart. May my life reflect faith, love, and forgiveness.

Day 1 — To the Holy Family

Jesus, Mary, and Joseph, bless my home.
Fill it with peace, love, and faith. Help me walk in unity and kindness.

Prayer

Jesus, Mary, and Joseph,
I give You my heart and soul.
Protect my family, guide our steps,
and make our home a dwelling of peace and grace.
Amen.

— Traditional Holy Family Prayer

Day 2 — To the Blessed Virgin Mary, Our Lady of Lourdes

Mother Mary, healer of the sick.
You comfort those who suffer. Intercede for us and bring us healing and peace.

Prayer

O ever-Immaculate Virgin,

Mother of Mercy, Health of the Sick,
Refuge of Sinners,
comfort me in my sorrows and obtain
for me healing,
according to Your Son's will.
Amen.

— *Prayer to Our Lady of Lourdes*

Day 3 — To the Holy Spirit, Giver of Courage

Holy Spirit, strengthen my heart.
Help me stand firm in faith and act
with courage and love.

Prayer

Come, Holy Spirit,
fill me with holy courage.
Let Your gifts of fortitude and wisdom
guide me through every challenge.
Amen.

— *Traditional Invocation to the Holy Spirit*

Day 4 — To Saint Blaise, Protector of Health

Saint Blaise, intercede for me.
Protect me from every illness of body and spirit,
and keep me strong in faith.

Prayer

O Blessed Saint Blaise,
hear my prayer.
Grant me health of throat and body,
and protect me from all harm.
Through your intercession,
may I always praise God with a grateful heart.
Amen.

— Traditional Blessing of Saint Blaise

Day 5 — To the Sacred Heart of Jesus

Jesus, Your Heart is my home.
Let Your love fill me with peace and joy.

Prayer

O Sacred Heart of Jesus,
I place my trust in You.
Grant me a heart like Yours—
humble, loving, and full of mercy.
Amen.

— *Devotion to the Sacred Heart*

Day 6 — To Saint Joseph, Protector of Families

Saint Joseph, humble and faithful.
Watch over our homes and lead us
closer to Jesus and Mary.

Prayer

O Glorious Saint Joseph,
protector of the Holy Family,
defend us in life and in death.
Keep us pure of heart and strong in
love. Amen.

— *Traditional Prayer to Saint Joseph*

Day 7 — To the Holy Spirit, Fire of Love

Holy Spirit, flame of divine love.
Ignite my heart and fill me with Your presence.

Prayer

Come, Holy Spirit,
enlighten my mind, enflame my heart,
and make me an instrument of Your love and truth.
Amen.

— *"Veni Sancte Spiritus"*

Day 8 — To the Immaculate Heart of Mary

Immaculate Heart of Mary, my refuge and joy.
Teach me to love purely and trust completely in God.

Prayer

O Immaculate Heart of Mary,
I give You my heart.

Keep it free from sin,
and fill it with peace and holiness.
Amen.

— Traditional Devotion to the Immaculate Heart of Mary

Day 9 — To the Divine Mercy of Jesus

Jesus, I trust in Your mercy.
You are my refuge and my hope.

Prayer

Eternal Father,
I offer You the Body and Blood, Soul
and Divinity of Your dearly beloved Son,
our Lord Jesus Christ, in atonement for
our sins and those of the whole world.
For the sake of our sorrowful passion.
Have mercy on us and the whole world.
Amen.

— From the Divine Mercy Chaplet

Day 10 — To Saint George, Defender of Faith

Saint George, brave soldier of Christ.
Grant me courage to face all trials and stand strong in faith.

Prayer

Saint George, warrior of God,
protect me from all evil and harm.
Give me strength to fight temptation
and remain faithful to Christ's love.
Amen.

— *Traditional Prayer to Saint George*

Day 11 — To Mother Mary, Destroyer of the Devil

Blessed Virgin Mary, mighty defender.
Crush the enemy beneath your feet and protect my soul with your light.

Prayer

O Mary, Immaculate Conqueror,
destroyer of the devil,

guard me with your mantle of grace,
and lead me safely to your Son.
Amen.

— *Traditional Marian Invocation*

Day 12 — To Jesus, Healer of the Broken-hearted

Jesus, my healer and comforter.
Heal my wounds, restore my peace, and renew my faith.

Prayer

O Jesus, Divine Physician, touch my heart and heal my body and spirit.
Grant me patience and faith in Your loving will.
Amen.

— *Healing Prayer*

Day 13 — To Saint Michael the Archangel

Saint Michael, defender of God's people. Guard me from all evil and keep my soul safe in God's care.

Prayer

Saint Michael the Archangel,
defend us in battle.
Be our protection against the wickedness and snares of the devil.
May God rebuke him, we humbly pray,
and do thou, O Prince of the Heavenly Host,
by the power of God,
cast into hell Satan and all evil spirits who prowl about the world seeking the ruin of souls.
Amen.

— Traditional Saint Michael Prayer

Day 14 — To the Sacred Heart of Jesus (Feast of Love)

Jesus, my heart rests in Yours.

Let my love be pure, patient, and kind.

Prayer

O Sacred Heart of Jesus,
teach me to love as You love—
forgiving, generous, and full of grace.
Let my heart reflect Your mercy.
Amen.

— Sacred Heart Devotion

Day 15 — Prayer for Serenity

Lord, fill me with peace and calm.

Teach me to trust Your will and rest in Your care.

Prayer

God, grant me the serenity
to accept the things I cannot change,
courage to change the things I can,

and wisdom to know the difference.
Amen.

— *Serenity Prayer*

Day 16 — To the Holy Spirit, Spirit of Truth

Holy Spirit, enlighten me.

Help me see truth, speak truth, and live in truth.

Prayer

Spirit of Truth,
open my eyes to see the goodness of God,
and guide me in honesty, humility, and peace.
Amen.

— *Traditional Holy Spirit Invocation*

FEBRUARY

Day 17 — To Saint Bernadette of Lourdes

Saint Bernadette, humble servant of Mary.
Teach me simplicity and faith in God's love.

Prayer
Saint Bernadette,
you found joy in prayer and patience in suffering.
Help me accept my crosses with peace and trust in Our Lady's intercession.
Amen.

— Traditional Prayer to Saint Bernadette

Day 18 — To the Holy Cross
O Cross of Christ, my victory.
Remind me of God's love and redeeming power.

Prayer
We adore You, O Christ, and we bless

You,
because by Your holy Cross You have redeemed the world.
Amen.

— *Traditional Stations of the Cross Prayer*

Day 19 — To Jesus, the Good Shepherd
Jesus, my shepherd and guide.
Lead me along Your path of peace and love.

Prayer
O Lord, my Shepherd,
guide me to green pastures of peace
and living waters of grace.
I shall not fear, for You are with me.
Amen.

— *Inspired by Psalm 23*

Day 20 — To Saint Peter, Keeper of Faith

Saint Peter, steadfast apostle.
Help me stay firm in faith and love for Christ.

Prayer
O Saint Peter,
rock upon whom the Church was built,
pray that my faith may never falter.
Guide me in truth and courage.
Amen.

— Traditional Prayer to Saint Peter

Day 21 — To Mother Mary, Our Lady of Fatima

Our Lady of Fatima, Queen of Peace.
Guide me in prayer and lead the world to conversion.

Prayer
O Most Holy Virgin Mary,
Queen of the Rosary and of Peace,

lead all souls to God.
May Your Immaculate Heart triumph.
Amen.

— *Fatima Prayer*

Day 22 — To the Holy Spirit, Breath of Life

Holy Spirit, renew me.

Fill me with Your breath of life and keep me steadfast in faith.

Prayer

Come, Holy Spirit, Creator blest,
and in our souls take up Your rest.
Fill us with grace and heavenly aid.
Amen.

— *Veni Creator Spiritus*

Day 23 — To the Eucharistic Heart of Jesus

Jesus, Bread of Life.
You dwell within me—strengthen my soul with Your grace.

Prayer

O Jesus, in the Most Blessed Sacrament, I adore You.
Stay with me, strengthen me, and fill me with Your peace.
Amen.

— *Eucharistic Adoration Prayer*

Day 24 — To the Guardian Angel

My guardian angel, faithful friend.
Stay by my side and keep me close to God.

Prayer

Angel of God, my guardian dear,
to whom His love commits me here,
ever this day be at my side,

to light and guard, to rule and guide.
Amen.

— *Guardian Angel Prayer*

Day 25 — To Saint Therese of Lisieux
Saint Therese, little flower of love.
Teach me to find God in small acts of kindness.

Prayer
O Saint Therese,
help me to trust God's plan in every moment
and to love with simplicity and joy.
Amen.

— *Traditional Prayer to Saint Therese*

Day 26 — To the Precious Blood of Jesus
Jesus, Your blood redeems and protects.
Wash me clean and make my heart new.

Prayer

By the Precious Blood of Jesus,
deliver me from evil and protect my
soul.
May I live in purity and grace.
Amen.

— *Devotion to the Precious Blood*

Day 27 — To Saint Gabriel the Archangel

Saint Gabriel, messenger of God.
Help me listen to God's voice and
respond with faith.

Prayer
Saint Gabriel,
bring me good news of God's love.
Help me live with courage and proclaim
His Word with joy.
Amen.

— *Prayer to Saint Gabriel the Archangel*

Day 28 — To Jesus, King of Mercy
Jesus, King of my heart.

Reign in me and make me a vessel of Your mercy.

Prayer

O Jesus, King of Mercy,
rule my heart and guide my soul.
Help me show compassion to others,
as You have shown to me.
Amen.

— Devotion to Christ the King

Day 29 — To the Holy Family (Leap Year Blessing)
Jesus, Mary, and Joseph, my holy family.

Be with me through every season of life.

Prayer

O Holy Family of Nazareth,
make my heart Your dwelling place.
Bless my family, keep us united,

and bring us closer to the heart of God.
Amen.

— Blessing for the Month of the Holy Family

MARCH

Month of Saint Joseph

Affirmation for the Month

In this month of Saint Joseph,
I walk with quiet strength, humble
faith, and trust in God's perfect timing.
Saint Joseph, protect my heart, guide
my steps, and lead me closer to Jesus
and Mary.

MARCH

Day 1 — To Saint Joseph, Guardian of the Redeemer
Saint Joseph, strong and faithful.
Teach me to trust God even when I do not understand His ways.

Prayer
O Saint Joseph,
Guardian of the Redeemer
and protector of the Holy Family,
watch over me as you watched over Jesus and Mary.
Help me live with courage, purity, and quiet faithfulness.
Amen.

— *Litany of Saint Joseph (inspired)*

Day 2 — To Jesus, the Light of the World
Jesus, be my light and guide.
Shine upon my path and lead me in truth.

Prayer

O Jesus, Light of the World,
remove all darkness from my heart.
Fill me with Your love,
and guide me in Your peace and
goodness. Amen.

— Traditional Invocation to Christ the Light

Day 3 — To the Holy Spirit, Spirit of Wisdom

Holy Spirit, enlighten my mind.
Grant me understanding, clarity, and peace.

Prayer

Come, Holy Spirit,
Spirit of Wisdom and Truth.
Guide my thoughts, inspire my choices,
and help me see all things with the eyes of God. Amen.

— Veni Sancte Spiritus (inspired)

Day 4 — To Mother Mary, Our Lady of Sorrows

Mother Mary, full of compassion and strength.
Teach me to remain faithful in moments of pain and uncertainty.
Help me surrender my worries to Jesus with trust and humility.

Prayer
O Mother of Sorrows,
you who stood faithfully beneath the Cross,
hold my heart in your gentle care.
Help me unite my struggles with Jesus,
and lead me always toward His love and mercy.
Amen.

— Traditional Devotion to Our Lady of Sorrows (inspired)

Day 5 — To Saint Joseph the Worker
Saint Joseph, humble worker and faithful protector.
Bless my efforts today. My labor, my plans, and my decisions.
Teach me to work with patience, dignity, and grace.

Prayer
O Saint Joseph,
model of all who labor, sanctify my work and guide my hands.
Help me offer every task, big or small, for the glory of God and the good of others. Amen.

— *Prayer to Saint Joseph the Worker (inspired)*

Day 6 — To Jesus, the Good Shepherd

Jesus, my Good Shepherd,
Lead me gently today.
When I am confused, guide me.

When I am afraid, comfort me.
When I am weak, strengthen me.

Prayer
Lord Jesus,
Good Shepherd who never abandons His flock, walk with me through this day. Hold me close to Your Heart and lead me along the path of peace. Amen.

— *Traditional Devotion to the Good Shepherd (inspired)*

Day 7 — To the Holy Spirit, Giver of Courage
Holy Spirit, my Strength and my Courage.
Fill my heart with holy boldness.
Help me face challenges with faith,
and trust Your power within me.

Prayer
Come, Holy Spirit, Giver of Courage,
remove all fear from my heart.

Fill me with confidence in God's love
and strengthen me in every good work.
Amen.

— *Veni Creator Spiritus (inspired)*

Day 8 — To Mother Mary, Our Lady of Fatima

Our Lady of Fatima, gentle and radiant Mother.
Teach me to pray with sincerity
and to love Jesus with all my heart.

Prayer
O Mary, Our Lady of Fatima,
turn my heart toward your Son.
Help me embrace prayer, penance, and peace.
Guide me always toward the light of God's mercy. Amen.

— *Fatima Devotion (inspired)*

Day 9 — To Jesus, Fountain of Mercy
Jesus, overflowing with mercy and compassion.

Wash my heart clean and fill me with the grace to begin again.

Prayer

O Jesus,
Fountain of endless mercy,
have mercy on me.
Cleanse my soul, renew my heart,
and draw me deeper into Your love.
Amen.

— *Divine Mercy Devotion (inspired)*

Day 10 — To the Guardian Angel
My Guardian Angel, faithful companion.

Stay close to me today
and guide every step I take.

Prayer

Angel of God,

my guardian dear,
to whom God's love commits me here,
ever this day be at my side,
to light and guard,
to rule and guide. Amen.

— *Traditional Guardian Angel Prayer*

Day 11 — To Saint Joseph, Pillar of Families

Saint Joseph, gentle protector of homes.
Watch over my family with loving care.
Unite us in peace, patience, and faith.

Prayer

O Saint Joseph, Pillar of Families,
guard our home with your fatherly
heart. Keep us safe from harm
and guide us in the ways of love and
unity. Amen.

— *Litany of Saint Joseph (inspired)*

Day 12 — To Saint Michael the Archangel

Saint Michael, mighty defender.
Stand with me in moments of temptation, fear,
and spiritual battle.

Prayer
Saint Michael the Archangel,
defend us in battle.
Be our protection against the wickedness and snares of the devil.
May God rebuke him, we humbly pray;
and do Thou, O Prince of the Heavenly Host,
by the power of God,
cast into hell Satan
and all the evil spirits
who prowl about the world
seeking the ruin of souls. Amen.

— Traditional St. Michael Prayer

Day 13 — To Jesus, My Peace

Jesus, Prince of Peace.
Calm every storm within me
and fill my heart with Your quiet
strength.

Prayer

O Jesus,
my Peace and my Rest,
settle my thoughts
and let Your presence surround me.
Help me trust You completely
in all things.
Amen.

— Traditional invocation (inspired)

Day 14 — The Fatima Prayer

O my Jesus, You are mercy itself.
Fill my heart with forgiveness and
compassion.

Prayer

O my Jesus, forgive us our sins,

save us from the fires of hell,
lead all souls to heaven,
especially those most in need of Your mercy.
Amen.

— *Fatima Prayer*

Day 15 — To God, the Source of Serenity

God, my refuge and peace.
Grant me courage, clarity, and calm.

Prayer

God, grant me the serenity
to accept the things I cannot change,
courage to change the things I can,
and wisdom to know the difference.
Amen.

— *Serenity Prayer*

Day 16 — To Saint Joseph, Protector of the Church

Saint Joseph, guardian and defender. Protect my faith from doubt and despair. Help me cling to Jesus with courage and trust.

Prayer

O Saint Joseph,
Protector of the Holy Church,
shield my heart from every attack of fear or confusion.
Strengthen my faith,
and lead me closer to Jesus and Mary.
Amen.

— Litany of Saint Joseph (inspired)

Day 17 — To Saint Patrick, Apostle of Ireland

Saint Patrick, faithful missionary and brave servant of God, fill my heart with courage to share God's love wherever I go.

Prayer

Christ with me, Christ before me, Christ behind me, Christ in me, Christ beneath me, Christ above me, Christ on my right, Christ on my left, Christ when I lie down, Christ when I sit down, Christ in the heart of every man who thinks of me, Christ in the mouth of every man who speaks of me,

Christ in the eye that sees me, Christ in the ear that hears me.

I arise today. Through a mighty strength, the invocation of the Trinity, Through a belief in the Threeness, Through a confession of the Oneness Of the Creator of creation. Amen.

— *St. Patrick prayer*

Day 18 — To Mother Mary, Star of the Sea

Mother Mary, Star of the Sea, guide my soul. Calm the waves within me and bring me safely to Jesus.

Prayer

O Mary, Star of the Sea,
light my way through every uncertainty.
Protect me from danger
and lead me always to your Son. Amen.

— Traditional Marian devotion (inspired)

Day 19 — Solemnity of Saint Joseph, Spouse of the Blessed Virgin Mary

Saint Joseph, chosen by God,
teach me humility, obedience, and strength of heart.

Prayer

Hail, Guardian of the Redeemer,
Spouse of the Blessed Virgin Mary.

To you God entrusted His only Son;
in you Mary placed her trust;
with you Christ became man.
Bless and protect me,
and help me grow in virtue and
holiness. Amen.

— *Official Prayer to Saint Joseph*

Day 20 — To Jesus, the Bread of Life

Jesus, You nourish and strengthen my soul. Fill me with Your presence and love.

Prayer

Lord Jesus, Bread of Life,
feed my heart with Your grace.
Sustain me, renew me,
and draw me deeper into Your Sacred Heart.
Amen.

— *Eucharistic devotion (inspired)*

Day 21 — To the Holy Spirit, Giver of Hope

Holy Spirit, lift my spirit.
Fill me with hope that does not fade
and faith that does not weaken.

Prayer

Come, Holy Spirit,
fill me with hope and holy desire.
Strengthen me when I grow weary
and remind me of God's unending love.
Amen.

— Inspired by the Pentecost Sequence

Day 22 — To Saint Gabriel the Archangel

Saint Gabriel, messenger of God.
Help me listen for God's voice
and say yes with courage and joy.

Prayer

Saint Gabriel,
holy messenger of the Lord,

open my ears to God's whisper
and guide me in doing His will
with faith and humility.
Amen.

— *Traditional Gabriel devotion (inspired)*

Day 23 — To Saint Joseph, Model of Patience

Saint Joseph, calm and faithful.
Teach me patience in moments of waiting.

Prayer

O Saint Joseph,
model of patient endurance,
help me trust God's timing
and stay faithful in every trial. Amen.

— *Litany of Saint Joseph (inspired)*

Day 24 — To the Blessed Trinity

Father, Son, and Holy Spirit — my God and my all.

Surround me with Your love and guide my heart.

Prayer

Glory be to the Father, and to the Son, and to the Holy Spirit.
As it was in the beginning, is now, and ever shall be, world without end. Amen.

— *Glory Be*

Day 25 — The Annunciation to Mother Mary

Mother Mary, full of grace and faith.
Help me say yes to God in my own life.

Prayer

Hail Mary, full of grace,
the Lord is with you.
Blessed are you among women,
and blessed is the fruit of your womb, Jesus.
Holy Mary, Mother of God,
pray for us sinners,

now and at the hour of our death.
Amen.

— *Hail Mary*

Day 26 — To Saint Joseph, Mirror of Charity

Saint Joseph, loving and generous of heart.
Teach me to love gently,
forgive freely,
and serve humbly.

Prayer

Saint Joseph,
Mirror of Charity,
reflect God's love into my heart.
Help me love others
as Jesus loves me. Amen.

— *Litany of Saint Joseph (inspired)*

Day 27 — To Saint George, Courageous Martyr

Saint George, brave witness of Christ.
Strengthen me in faith and help me resist the enemy's attacks.

Prayer

O Saint George,
victorious soldier of Christ,
defend me from all evil
and give me courage
to stand firm in God's truth.
Amen.

— Traditional St. George devotion (inspired)

Day 28 — To Jesus, the Sacred Heart

Sacred Heart of Jesus, burning with love for me.
Heal my wounds and fill me with Your peace.

Prayer

O Sacred Heart of Jesus,

I place all my trust in You.
Make my heart like Yours—
gentle, humble, and full of mercy.
Amen.

— *Sacred Heart devotion*

Day 29 — To the Holy Spirit, Spirit of Renewal

Holy Spirit, refresh my heart.
Renew my strength
and breathe new life into my soul.

Prayer
Come, Holy Spirit,
renew the face of my heart.
Revive my spirit
and guide me in the way of holiness.
Amen.

— *Inspired by Psalm 104 and Pentecost prayer*

Day 30 — To Saint Joseph, Terror of Demons

Saint Joseph, mighty protector.
Stand guard over my soul
and keep all evil far from me.

Prayer

Saint Joseph, Terror of Demons,
drive away every darkness and fear.
Protect me with your strong and gentle heart,
and lead me safely to Jesus.
Amen.

— *From the Litany of Saint Joseph*

Day 31 — To Jesus, My Redeemer

Jesus, my Savior and Redeemer.
Thank You for carrying me through this month.
Help me begin the next with faith and love.

MARCH

Prayer

Lord Jesus,

Redeemer of my soul,

purify my heart

and strengthen my spirit.

Stay with me always

and lead me in Your everlasting mercy.

Amen.

— Traditional devotion (inspired)

APRIL

Month of the Holy Eucharist

Affirmation for the Month

In this month of the Holy Eucharist, I draw closer to Jesus, present in His Body and Blood. Lord, renew my heart with Your mercy, restore my hope, and make me a witness of Your risen love.

APRIL

Day 1 — To Jesus in the Holy Eucharist
Jesus, Bread of Life,
nourish my soul and strengthen my faith.

Prayer

O Jesus, truly present in the Holy Eucharist,
I adore You, love You, and thank You.
Remain with me, Lord, and fill my heart with Your grace and peace.
Amen.

— *Prayer of Eucharistic Adoration (inspired)*

Day 2 — To the Risen Christ
Jesus, my Risen Lord,
fill me with Easter joy and new life.

Prayer

O Risen Christ,
You conquered sin, death, and fear.
Raise me up with You,
renew my spirit,

and lead me into the fullness of Your light.
Amen.

— *Easter Morning Prayer (inspired)*

Day 3 — To the Holy Spirit, Bringer of Renewal

Holy Spirit, renew my heart
and restore what has grown weary.

Prayer

Come, Holy Spirit,
Breath of the Risen Lord.
Refresh my soul,
renew my strength,
and fill me with hope that never fades.
Amen.

— *Spirit of Renewal Invocation*

Day 4 — To the Sacred Heart of Jesus

Jesus, gentle and loving Heart,
draw me into Your mercy.

Prayer

O Sacred Heart of Jesus,
fountain of love and compassion,
heal my wounds,
calm my fears,
and keep me close to Your heart.
Amen.

— *Sacred Heart Devotion*

Day 5 — To Mary, Mother of the Risen Lord

Mother Mary,
gentle Queen of Heaven,
guide me to your Son.

Prayer

Hail Mary, full of grace,
the Lord is with thee;
blessed art thou among women,
and blessed is the fruit of thy womb,
Jesus.
Holy Mary, Mother of God,

pray for us sinners,
now and at the hour of our death.
Amen.

— *Hail Mary (Traditional)*

Day 6 — Holy Spirit Prayer of Saint Augustine

Holy Spirit, make my thoughts, actions, and heart holy.

Prayer

Breathe in me, O Holy Spirit, That my thoughts may all be holy. Act in me, O Holy Spirit, That my work, too, may be holy. Draw my heart, O Holy Spirit, That I love but what is holy. Strengthen me, O Holy Spirit, To defend all that is holy. Guard me, then, O Holy Spirit, That I always may be holy. Amen

— *Holy Spirit Prayer of Saint Augustine*

Day 7 — To Jesus, the Good Shepherd

Jesus, Good Shepherd,

lead me and keep me close to You.

Prayer

O Good Shepherd, you know me,

love me, and call me by name.

Guide my steps, protect my heart,

and grant me the grace to follow You

always.

Amen.

— *Psalm 23 & Good Shepherd Devotion (inspired)*

Day 8 — To the Holy Spirit, Spirit of Truth

Holy Spirit, fill me with truth, wisdom, and clarity.

Prayer

Come, Spirit of Truth,

open my eyes and heart.

Help me walk in honesty,

kindness, and the light of God's wisdom.
Amen.

— *Veni Creator Spiritus (inspired)*

Day 9 — To the Divine Mercy of Jesus

Jesus, Divine Mercy,
I trust in You.

Prayer

O Blood and Water,
which gushed forth from the Heart of Jesus as a fountain of mercy for us,
I trust in You!
Embrace me with Your compassion, forgive my sins, and fill me with Your peace.
Amen.

— *Divine Mercy Prayer (St. Faustina)*

Day 10 — To Saint Joseph, Protector of Families

Saint Joseph, guardian and protector, watch over my family.

Prayer

O Saint Joseph,
faithful protector of the Church and of families, guard us from harm,
strengthen our faith, and keep our hearts united in love.
Amen.

— *Saint Joseph Devotion*

Day 11 — To the Precious Blood of Jesus

Jesus, wash me in Your Precious Blood and make me new.

Prayer

O Precious Blood of Jesus, flow over my soul, cleanse me of all sin, and protect me from all evil. You are my hope and salvation. Amen.

— *Litany of the Precious Blood (inspired)*

Day 12 — To the Guardian Angel

God's angels watch over me with love.
I am never alone.

Prayer

Angel of God, my guardian dear,
to whom God's love commits me here,
ever this day be at my side,
to light and guard,
to rule and guide.
Amen.

— *Traditional Guardian Angel Prayer*

Day 13 — To Mary, Queen of Peace

Mother Mary, Queen of Peace,
calm my mind and soften my heart.

Prayer

O Queen of Peace,

bring peace to my heart,
peace to my home,
and peace to the world.
Lead me gently to Jesus.
Amen.

— Regina Pacis Invocation

Day 14 — To Jesus, the Healer

Jesus, Divine Healer,
touch my heart with Your healing love.

Prayer

Lord Jesus,
You healed the sick
and comforted the weary.
Heal my wounds,
strengthen my spirit,
and restore my hope.
Amen.

— Healing Prayer of Jesus (inspired)

Day 15 — To the Holy Spirit, Giver of Courage

Holy Spirit,
fill me with bravery and strength.

Prayer

Come, Holy Spirit,
give me courage to face my challenges.
Fill my heart with confidence,
trust,
and unwavering faith.
Amen.

— Pentecost Prayer (inspired)

Day 16 — To the Cross of Christ

The Cross of Jesus
is my strength and hope.

Prayer

O Holy Cross,
sign of love and sacrifice,
remind me of Jesus' victory
over sin and death.

Help me carry my burdens
with patience and trust.
Amen.

— *Sign of the Cross Devotion*

Day 17 — To Saint Patrick, Apostle of Ireland

Saint Patrick, faithful missionary and
brave servant of God.
Fill my heart with courage
to share God's love wherever I go.

Prayer

Christ with me, Christ before me, Christ behind me, Christ in me, Christ beneath me, Christ above me, Christ on my right, Christ on my left, Christ when I lie down, Christ when I sit down, Christ in the heart of every man who thinks of me, Christ in the mouth of every man who speaks of me,

Christ in the eye that sees me, Christ in the ear that hears me.

I arise today.

Through a mighty strength, the invocation of the Trinity,

Through a belief in the Threeness,

Through a confession of the Oneness

Of the Creator of creation.

Amen.

— *St. Patrick prayer*

Day 18 — To the Immaculate Heart of Mary

Mother Mary,
pure and loving heart,
draw me close to Jesus.

Prayer

O Immaculate Heart of Mary,
be my refuge and my strength.

Guide me in purity, humility, and trust.
Lead me always to your Son.
Amen.

— *Immaculate Heart Devotion*

Day 19 — To Saint George, Defender of Faith

Saint George, brave warrior of Christ,
strengthen my courage.

Prayer

Saint George, victorious over evil,
help me stand firm in faith.
Protect me from all fear and guide me
in God's strength.
Amen.

— *St. George Devotion (traditional)*

Day 20 — To Jesus, Prince of Peace

Jesus, Prince of Peace,
calm my heart and guide my steps.

Prayer

O Prince of Peace, bring stillness to my
mind, gentleness to my heart,
and harmony to my life.
Fill me with Your peace
that surpasses all understanding.
Amen.

— *Peace Prayer (inspired)*

Day 21 — To the Holy Spirit, Fire of Love

Holy Spirit, ignite my heart with love for God.

Prayer

Come, Holy Spirit,
Fire of Divine Love.
Burn away all fear, selfishness, and doubt. Fill me with Your warmth and joy. Amen.

— *Holy Spirit Fire Devotion*

Day 22 — To Mary, Mother of Hope

Mary, guide us in moments of doubt and lead our hearts back to trust in God's loving plan.

Prayer

O Mary, Mother of Hope,
guide us when our hearts feel unsure,
strengthen our trust in God's plan,
and help us walk with faith, courage,
and peace. Stay close when doubts
arise, lift our spirits when we grow
weary, teach us to wait with patience
and love, and lead us always toward
your Son. Amen.

— *Marian Devotion*

Day 23 — To Mary, Undoer of Knots

Mother Mary, undo the knots in my life and bring me peace.

Prayer

Mother Mary, Undoer of Knots,

intercede for me.
Untangle the problems I cannot solve,
and lead me to the peace of Christ.
Amen.

— *Mary Undoer of Knots Devotion*

Day 24 — To the Saints
All you holy saints of God,
pray for me.

Prayer
Holy Saints of God,
faithful servants of Christ,
surround me with your prayers.
Help me live with humility,
kindness, and a grateful heart. Amen.

— *Litany of the Saints (inspired)*

Day 25 — To Jesus, the King of Glory
Jesus, my King and my Lord,
reign in my heart.

APRIL

Prayer
O King of Glory, rule my heart with love, truth, and mercy. Guide my thoughts and lead me ever closer to You. Amen.

— *Christ the King Devotion*

Day 26 — To the Holy Spirit, Comforter
Holy Spirit, comfort my heart
and fill me with hope.

Prayer
Come, Holy Spirit,
Comforter and Friend.
Lift my burdens,
soothe my worries,
and fill my soul with peace. Amen.

— *Holy Spirit Consoler Invocation*

Day 27 — To Saint Joseph the Worker
Saint Joseph, teach me to work with love, patience, and purpose.

Prayer

O Saint Joseph the Worker,
model of diligence and humility,
bless the work of my hands
and the intentions of my heart.
Help me honour God in all I do. Amen.

— *Prayer to St. Joseph the Worker*

Day 28 — To the Holy Eucharist (Act of Love)

Jesus in the Eucharist,
You are my life and my joy.

Prayer

My Jesus, I believe that You are truly
present in the Holy Eucharist.
I love You above all things
and desire to receive You into my heart.
Remain with me, Lord.
Amen.

— *Act of Spiritual Communion (traditional, adapted)*

Day 29 — To Mary Magdalene, Witness of the Resurrection

Saint Mary Magdalene, teach me to love Jesus boldly.

Prayer

Saint Mary Magdalene,
faithful witness of Christ's Resurrection,
pray for me. Help me seek Jesus with a sincere heart and follow Him with perseverance.
Amen.

— *St. Mary Magdalene Devotion*

Day 30 — To the Most Holy Trinity, Source of All Grace

Holy Trinity, guide me to walk in Your light.

Prayer

Most Holy Trinity,
Father, Son, and Holy Spirit,
I turn to You in faith and humility.

Lead me in wisdom, strengthen me in weakness,
and fill my heart with Your peace and courage.
Help me to live each day reflecting Your love
and trusting completely in Your divine plan.
Amen.

— Holy Trinity Devotion

MAY

Month of the

Blessed Virgin Mary

Affirmation for the Month

In this month of Mother Mary,
I entrust my heart to her gentle care.
Mary, Mother of Mercy, guide my
thoughts, lead me closer to Jesus,
and help me live with humility, faith,
and love.

Day 1 — To Mary, Mother of God

Mary, full of grace, teach me to say yes to God with trust.

Prayer

Hail Mary, full of grace,
the Lord is with thee;
blessed art thou among women,
and blessed is the fruit of thy womb, Jesus.
Holy Mary, Mother of God,
pray for us sinners,
now and at the hour of our death.
Amen.

— *Hail Mary (Traditional)*

Day 2 — To Mary, Queen of Heaven

Mother Mary, Queen of Heaven,
intercede for me and guide my steps.

Prayer

O Mary, Queen of Heaven,
look kindly upon me, your child.

Help me grow in faith, hope, and love,
and lead me always to your Son.
Amen.

— *Marian Devotion (inspired)*

Day 3 — To the Holy Spirit, Spirit of Guidance

Holy Spirit, illuminate my mind and heart.

Prayer

Come, Holy Spirit,
Guide and Teacher of all hearts.
Help me discern God's will, strengthen my faith, and lead me gently along the path of holiness.

Amen.

— *Veni Sancte Spiritus (inspired)*

Day 4 — To Mother Mary, Our Lady of Fatima

Mary, gentle Mother, teach me to pray with love and devotion.

Prayer

O Mary, Our Lady of Fatima,
help me pray the Rosary faithfully,
keep my heart pure, and lead me closer to Jesus. Amen.

— *Fatima Devotion (inspired)*

Day 5 — To Jesus, Divine Mercy

Jesus, mercy itself, have compassion on my soul.

Prayer

O Blood and Water, which gushed forth from the Heart of Jesus as a fountain of mercy for us, I trust in You! Forgive my sins and fill me with Your peace. Amen.

— *Divine Mercy Prayer (St. Faustina)*

Day 6 — To Saint Joseph, Guardian of the Redeemer

Saint Joseph, protector and guide,
teach me humility and faithfulness.

Prayer

O Saint Joseph,
guardian of Jesus and Mary,
watch over me and my loved ones.
Help me live with quiet courage,
patience, and trust in God's plan.
Amen.

— *Litany of Saint Joseph (inspired)*

Day 7 — To the Guardian Angel

God's angels watch over me with love.
I am never alone.

Prayer

Angel of God, my guardian dear,
to whom God's love commits me here,
ever be at my side,
to light and guard,

to rule and guide.
Amen.

— *Traditional Guardian Angel Prayer*

Day 8 — To Mary, Mother of Sorrows

Mother Mary, comforter of the afflicted,
teach me to trust Jesus in sorrow.

Prayer

O Mother of Sorrows,
help me unite my sufferings with Jesus' love.
Give me patience, courage,
and hope in God's mercy.
Amen.

— *Devotion to Our Lady of Sorrows*

Day 9 — To Saint Michael the Archangel

Saint Michael, defender of faith,
protect me from evil.

Prayer

Saint Michael the Archangel,
defend us in battle.
Be our protection against the wickedness
and snares of the devil.
Amen.

— *Traditional St. Michael Prayer*

Day 10 — To Jesus, the Good Shepherd

Jesus, my Shepherd,
guide my steps and protect my heart.

Prayer

O Good Shepherd,
lead me beside still waters,
restore my soul,
and keep me close to Your Sacred Heart.
Amen.

— *Psalm 23 & Good Shepherd Devotion (inspired)*

Day 11 — To the Holy Spirit, Spirit of Wisdom

Holy Spirit, fill my heart with understanding.

Prayer

Come, Holy Spirit,
Spirit of Wisdom,
guide my thoughts,
illuminate my mind,
and lead me in God's truth.
Amen.

— *Veni Sancte Spiritus (inspired)*

Day 12 — To Mary, Queen of Peace

Mother Mary, bring peace to my heart and home.

Prayer

O Queen of Peace,
soften my heart,
calm my mind,

and lead me always to Jesus.
Amen.

— *Regina Pacis Devotion*

Day 13 — To Saint Joseph, Model of Workers

Saint Joseph, teach me to work
faithfully and humbly.

Prayer

O Saint Joseph,
model of diligence and humility,
bless my work and guide my efforts.
Help me honor God in all I do.
Amen.

— *Prayer to Saint Joseph the Worker*

Day 14 — To Jesus, the Lamb of God

Jesus, Lamb of God,
have mercy on me.

Prayer

Lamb of God,

You take away the sins of the world:
have mercy on us.
Lamb of God,
grant us peace.
Amen.

— *Agnus Dei (Traditional)*

Day 15 — To Mary, Undoer of Knots

Mother Mary, untangle the problems in my life.

Prayer

Mother Mary, Undoer of Knots,
intercede for me with your Son.
Bring clarity, peace, and grace
to my heart and decisions.
Amen.

— *Mary Undoer of Knots Devotion*

Day 16 — To Saint George, Defender of Faith

Saint George, courageous soldier of Christ,
strengthen my faith and courage.

Prayer

O Saint George,
defend me from all fear,
help me stand firm in God's truth,
and inspire me to live with courage.
Amen.

— Traditional St. George Devotion

Day 17 — To Jesus, Sacred Heart

Jesus, Sacred Heart,
fill me with love and mercy.

Prayer

O Sacred Heart of Jesus,
I trust in You.
Heal my soul, strengthen my heart,

and let Your love shine through me.
Amen.

— *Sacred Heart Devotion*

Day 18 — To the Holy Spirit, Comforter

Holy Spirit, console me and fill me with peace.

Prayer

Come, Holy Spirit,
Comforter and Guide.
Soothe my worries,
renew my strength,
and dwell within me always.
Amen.

— *Holy Spirit Consoler Invocation*

Day 19 — To the Guardian Angel

My Guardian Angel, guide me and keep me safe.

Prayer

Angel of God, my guardian dear,

to whom God's love commits me here,
ever be at my side, to light and guard,
to rule and guide.
Amen.

— *Traditional Guardian Angel Prayer*

Day 20 — To Mary, Mother of Mercy

Mother Mary, teach me to show mercy to others.

Prayer

O Mother of Mercy, fill my heart with compassion.

Help me forgive, love, and serve, following the example of your Son.
Amen.

— *Marian Devotion*

Day 21 — To Jesus, Light of the World

Jesus, shine in my life and guide my path.

Prayer

O Jesus, Light of the World,
illuminate my soul,
show me the way to Your love,
and keep me close to You always.
Amen.

— *Traditional Invocation to Christ the Light*

Day 22 — To Saint Joseph, Pillar of Families

Saint Joseph, guide and protect my family.

Prayer

O Saint Joseph,
pillar of all families,
guard our hearts,
strengthen our bonds,
and lead us closer to Jesus and Mary.
Amen.

— *Litany of Saint Joseph (inspired)*

Day 23 — To the Holy Spirit, Spirit of Hope

Holy Spirit, fill me with hope and joy.

Prayer

Come, Holy Spirit,
Spirit of Hope, lift my heart,
strengthen my faith, and renew my
trust in God's plan. Amen.

— *Pentecost Prayer*

Day 24 — To Mary, Star of the Sea

Mother Mary, guide me safely through life's storms.

Prayer

O Mary, Star of the Sea,
light my way and protect me.
Lead me always to Jesus,
my safe harbor and my peace.
Amen.

— *Marian Devotion (inspired)*

Day 25 — To Jesus, Risen Lord

Jesus, Risen Lord,

fill me with the joy of Your resurrection.

Prayer

O Risen Christ,

raise my spirit from fear and sadness.

Help me walk in Your light,

and share Your love with all. Amen.

— Easter Devotion (inspired)

Day 26 — To Saint Michael the Archangel

Saint Michael, defend me from evil and guide me in truth.

Prayer

Saint Michael the Archangel,

protect me from all harm,

and lead me in courage, faith, and righteousness. Amen.

— Traditional St. Michael Prayer

Day 27 — To Jesus, Divine Healer

Jesus, heal my heart, body, and soul.

Prayer

O Jesus, Divine Healer,
touch every wound within me, restore
my health, and fill me with Your peace
and mercy. Amen.

— *Healing Prayer (inspired)*

Day 28 — To the Holy Spirit, Fire of Love

Holy Spirit, ignite my heart with zeal and devotion.

Prayer

Come, Holy Spirit, holy fire of love.
Burn away my selfishness,
renew my faith,
and draw me closer to God.
Amen.

— *Holy Spirit Devotion*

Day 29 — To Mary, Our Lady of Grace

Mother Mary, bless me with Your guidance and protection.

Prayer

O Mary, Our Lady of Grace,
cover me with your mantle,
guide my choices,
and lead me safely to Jesus. Amen.

— Traditional Marian Devotion

Day 30 — To Jesus, Bread of Life

Jesus, nourish my soul with Your presence.

Prayer

O Jesus, Bread of Life,
feed my soul with Your grace.
Strengthen my faith, renew my hope,
and let me live in Your love always. Amen.

— Eucharistic Devotion (inspired)

Day 31 — To the Blessed Trinity

Father, Son, and Holy Spirit,

I adore You and give You my heart.

Prayer

Glory be to the Father,

and to the Son,

and to the Holy Spirit,

as it was in the beginning,

is now,

and ever shall be,

world without end.

Amen.

— Glory Be

JUNE

Month of the Sacred Heart / Holy Eucharist

Affirmation for the Month

In this month of the Sacred Heart,
I open my heart to Jesus' love.
Lord, inflame me with Your mercy,
guide me with Your compassion, and
help me serve others with Your heart.

JUNE

Day 1 — To the Sacred Heart of Jesus

Jesus, Sacred Heart,

fill my heart with love and mercy.

Prayer

O Sacred Heart of Jesus,

I trust in Your infinite love.

Teach me to love as You love,

forgive as You forgive,

and follow You with a faithful heart.

Amen.

— *Sacred Heart Devotion*

Day 2 — To Jesus in the Holy Eucharist

Jesus, Bread of Life,

nourish my soul with Your presence.

Prayer

O Jesus, truly present in the Holy Eucharist,

I adore You and receive You with love.

Strengthen my faith,

fill me with Your grace,

and help me always live in union with You.
Amen.

— *Eucharistic Adoration Prayer (inspired*

Day 3 — To the Holy Spirit, Spirit of Love

Holy Spirit,
come and fill me with Your fire.

Prayer

Come, Holy Spirit,
Spirit of Love and Consolation.
Inflame my heart with zeal for God,
renew my soul with courage,
and guide me to live in holiness.
Amen.

— *Invocation to the Holy Spirit*

Day 4 — To Heavenly Father, Divine Healer

Heavenly Father, Divine Healer,
restore my soul and spirit.

Prayer

Loving Father, touch me now with your healing hands, for I believe that your will is for me to be well in mind, body, soul and spirit. Cover me with the most precious blood of your Son, our Lord, Jesus Christ from the top of my head to the soles of my feet.

— From the Prayer attributed to St. Padre Pio

Day 5 — To the Holy Spirit, Giver of Strength

Holy Spirit,
grant me courage to face life's challenges.

Prayer

Come, Holy Spirit, and from your celestial home, shed a ray of light divine. Come, Father of the poor, come, giver of all gifts, come, light of our hearts.

You are the best of comforters, the soul's most welcome guest, and sweet refreshment. You are sweet rest in labour, coolness in heat, and solace in sorrow.

O most blessed Light, fill the innermost hearts of your faithful. Without your grace, there is nothing in us that is not harmful.

Cleanse what is sordid, water what is arid, heal what is wounded. Bend what is rigid, warm what is cold, direct what is deviant.

Give to your faithful who trust in you
the sevenfold gifts. Grant the reward of
virtue, grant the deliverance of
salvation, and grant eternal joy.

Amen.

— *Veni Sancte Spiritus*

Day 6 — To Mary, Mother of Mercy

Mother Mary,
help me forgive and love with a pure
heart.

Prayer

O Mother of Mercy,
teach me to forgive as Jesus forgives,
to love as You love,
and to trust always in God's plan.
Amen.

— *Marian Devotion (inspired)*

Day 7 — To the Guardian Angel

My Guardian Angel,

guide me, protect me, and keep me safe.

Prayer

Angel of God, my guardian dear,

to whom God's love commits me here,

ever be at my side,

to light and guard,

to rule and guide.

Amen.

— *Traditional Guardian Angel Prayer*

Day 8 — To Saint Joseph, Protector of Families

Saint Joseph,

watch over my loved ones and home.

Prayer

O Saint Joseph, faithful protector,

guide our hearts in love,

keep us safe from harm,

and teach us trust and patience in God. Amen.

— *Litany of Saint Joseph (inspired)Day 9 — To Jesus, Prince of Peace*

Day 9 — To Jesus, Prince of Peace

Jesus, bring calm to my heart and life.

Prayer

Lord Jesus Christ, who are called the Prince of Peace, who are Yourself our peace and reconciliation, who so often said, "Peace to you" – please grant us peace.

Make all men and women witnesses of truth, justice and brotherly love. Banish from their hearts whatever might endanger peace. Enlighten our rulers that they may guarantee and defend the great gift of peace.

May all peoples on the earth become as brothers and sisters.

May longed-for peace blossom forth and reign always over us all. Amen.

— *Prayer for Peace, St. John Paul II*

Day 10 — To the Holy Spirit, Comforter

Holy Spirit,

console me and fill me with joy.

Prayer

Come, Holy Spirit,

Comforter of hearts,

renew my spirit,

lift my worries,

and fill me with Your joy and peace.

Amen.

— *Holy Spirit Devotion*

Day 11 — To Mary, Queen of Heaven

Mother Mary,

guide my decisions and bless my path.

JUNE

Prayer

O Mary, Queen of Heaven,
lead me with wisdom,
protect me with Your grace,
and draw me closer to Jesus each day.
Amen.

— *Marian Devotion*

Day 12 — To Jesus, Light of the World

Jesus, shine in my life and show me
Your way.

Prayer

O Jesus, Light of the World,
illuminate my thoughts,
guide my actions,
and lead me in Your truth and love.
Amen.

— *Traditional Invccation to Christ the Light*

Day 13 — To Saint Michael the Archangel

Saint Michael, defender of faith,
protect me from evil.

Prayer

Saint Michael the Archangel,
defend me in battle,
protect me from harm,
and strengthen me to live in courage
and faith.
Amen.

— *Traditional St. Michael Prayer*

Day 14 — To Mary, Undoer of Knots

Mother Mary,
untangle the difficulties in my life.

Prayer

Mother Mary, Undoer of Knots,
intercede for me before Jesus.
Bring peace, clarity, and grace,

and help me trust in God's plan.
Amen.

— *Mary Undoer of Knots Devotion*

Day 15 — To Jesus, the Good Shepherd
Jesus, guide me and keep me close to You.

Prayer
O Good Shepherd,
lead me beside still waters,
restore my soul,
and keep me in Your love and
protection.
Amen.
— *Psalm 23 & Good Shepherd Devotion (inspired)*

Day 16 — To the Holy Spirit, Spirit of Wisdom
Holy Spirit, grant me clarity and understanding.

Prayer

Come, Holy Spirit, and from your celestial home, shed a ray of light divine. Come, Father of the poor, come, giver of all gifts, come, light of our hearts. You are the best of comforters, the soul's most welcome guest, and sweet refreshment. You are sweet rest in labour, coolness in heat, and solace in sorrow.

O most blessed Light, fill the innermost hearts of your faithful. Without your grace, there is nothing in us that is not harmful. Cleanse what is sordid, water what is arid, heal what is wounded. Bend what is rigid, warm what is cold, direct what is deviant.

Give to your faithful who trust in you the sevenfold gifts. Grant the reward of virtue, grant the deliverance of salvation, and grant eternal joy.

Amen.

— *Veni Sancte Spiritus*

Day 17 — To Jesus, Divine Mercy

Jesus, I trust in Your mercy.

Prayer

O Blood and Water,
which gushed from the Heart of Jesus,
forgive my sins,
restore my hope,
and fill me with Your endless mercy.
Amen.

— *Divine Mercy Prayer (St. Faustina)*

Day 18 — To Saint George, Defender of Faith

Saint George, give me courage and strength.

Prayer

Saint George,

brave warrior of Christ,

protect me from fear,

help me stand firm in faith,

and live boldly in God's truth.

Amen.

— *St. George Devotion (traditional)*

Day 19 — To Mary, Mother of the Church

Mother Mary,

lead me to deeper love of Christ.

Prayer

O Mother of the Church,

guide me with your gentle hand,

teach me humility, patience, and faith,

and draw me closer to Jesus.

Amen.

— *Marian Devotion (inspired)*

Day 20 — To Jesus, Healer of the Sick

Jesus, heal my body, mind, and soul.

Prayer

O Jesus, Divine Healer,
touch my body with Your grace,
renew my spirit,
and restore me to wholeness.
Amen.

— *Healing Prayer (inspired)*

Day 21 — To the Holy Spirit, Spirit of Courage

Holy Spirit, strengthen me in trials.

Prayer

Come, Holy Spirit,
Spirit of courage and fortitude.
Help me face challenges with trust,
stand firm in faith,
and act with boldness in God's love.
Amen.

— Pentecost Prayer (inspired)

Day 22 — To Mary, Star of the Sea

Mother Mary, guide me through life's storms.

Prayer

O Mary, Star of the Sea,
light my way,
protect me from danger,
and bring me safely to Jesus.
Amen.

— Marian Devotion

Day 23 — To Jesus, Prince of Peace

Jesus, calm my fears and renew my hope.

Prayer

O Prince of Peace,
still my heart,
restore my courage,

and help me carry Your love to others. Amen.

— *Peace Prayer (inspired)*

Day 24 — To Saint Joseph, Pillar of Families

Saint Joseph, protect and strengthen my family.

Prayer

Gracious Saint Joseph, protect me and my family from all evil as you did the Holy Family. Kindly keep us ever united in the love of Christ, ever fervent in imitation of the virtue of our Blessed Lady, your sinless spouse, and always faithful in devotion to you. Amen.

— *Prayer to Saint Joseph*

Day 25 — To the Guardian Angel

Guardian Angel, watch over me and guide my choices.

Prayer

Angel of God, my guardian dear,
to whom God's love commits me here,
ever be at my side,
to light and guard,
to rule and guide.
Amen.

— Traditional Guardian Angel Prayer

Day 26 — To Christ, My Refuge and Strength

Jesus, draw me close and keep me in Your loving protection.

Prayer

Soul of Christ, sanctify me,
Body of Christ, save me,
Blood of Christ, inebriate me,
Water from the side of Christ, wash me,
Passion of Christ, strengthen me,
O good Jesus, hear me.
Hide me within your wounds,

keep me close to you,
defend me from the evil enemy,
call me at the hour of my death,
and bid me to come to you,
to praise you with your saints,
forever and ever. Amen.

— *Anima Christi*

Day 27 — To the Lord, My Protector

Lord, guide my steps and keep all in my care safe.

Prayer

Grant me, O Lord, a steady hand and watchful eye.
That no one shall be hurt as I pass by.
You gave life, I pray no act of mine may take away or mar that gift of thine.
Shelter those, dear Lord, who bear my company, from the evils of fire and all calamity. Teach me, to use my car for others need; Nor miss through love of

undue speed The beauty of the world; that thus I may with joy and courtesy go on my way. St. Christopher, holy patron of travellers, protect me and lead me safely to my destiny. Amen

— *Prayer to Saint Christopher*

Day 28 — To the Holy Spirit, Fire of Love

Holy Spirit, inflame my heart with zeal for God.

Prayer

Come, Holy Spirit,
holy fire of love,
burn away fear,
renew my faith,
and guide me in Your ways.
Amen.

— *Holy Spirit Devotion*

Day 29 — To Mary, Undoer of Knots

Mother Mary, help me overcome difficulties.

Prayer

Mother Mary, Undoer of Knots,
untangle the challenges in my life,
bring clarity and peace,
and lead me always to Jesus.
Amen.

— *Mary Undoer of Knots Devotion*

Day 30 —To Jesus, My Lord and All

Jesus, I entrust everything into Your loving hands.

Prayer

Lord Jesus Christ, take all my freedom, my understanding, and my will. All that I have and cherish that you have given to me. I surrender it all to be guided by your will. Your love and your grace are wealth is enough for me. Give me these,

Lord Jesus, and I ask for nothing more. Amen.

— *Prayer of Surrender*

JULY

Month of the Most Precious Blood of Jesus

Affirmation for the Month

In this month of the Precious Blood,
I open my heart to Jesus' saving love.
Lord, wash me clean with Your mercy,
fill me with courage, strength, and
compassion, and guide me in Your
truth.

Day 1 — To Jesus, Redeemer of Souls

Jesus, Precious Blood,

cleanse my heart and soul.

Prayer

O Jesus, Redeemer of souls,

by Your Most Precious Blood,

forgive my sins, heal my wounds,

and fill me with Your love and mercy.

Amen.

— Devotion to the Precious Blood (Traditional / inspired)

Day 2 — To the Holy Spirit, Spirit of Courage

Holy Spirit,

fill me with strength to follow Jesus.

Prayer

Come, Holy Spirit,

Spirit of courage and fortitude.

Strengthen my heart,

guide my decisions,

and help me walk boldly in God's ways.
Amen.

— *Pentecost Prayer (inspired)*

Day 3 — To Mary, Mother of Sorrows

Mother Mary, help me unite my sufferings with Jesus' love.

Prayer

O Mother of Sorrows,
comfort me in my trials,
teach me patience and hope,
and lead me closer to the heart of Jesus.
Amen.

— *Devotion to Our Lady of Sorrows*

Day 4 — To Jesus, the Perfume of Love and Sacrifice

Jesus, fill me with Your love, that my life may carry Your fragrance to the world.

Prayer

Help me to spread your fragrance everywhere I go - let me preach you without preaching, not by words but by my example - by the catching force, the sympathetic influence of what I do, the evident fullness of the love my heart bears to you. Amen

- The Fragrance of Christ

Day 5 — To Mary, Queen of Heaven

Mother Mary,
guide my decisions and bless my path.

Prayer
O Mary, Queen of Heaven,
lead me with wisdom,
protect me with Your grace,
and draw me closer to Jesus each day.
Amen.

— Marian Devotion

Day 6 — To the Holy Spirit, Spirit of Wisdom

Holy Spirit,

enlighten my mind and heart.

Prayer

Come, Holy Spirit,

Spirit of Wisdom,

guide my thoughts,

inspire my choices,

and help me live in God's truth.

Amen.

— *Veni Sancte Spiritus (inspired)*

Day 7 — To Saint Joseph, Protector of Families

Saint Joseph, watch over my loved ones and home.

Prayer

Hail, Joseph, image of the Eternal Father;

Hail, Joseph, guardian of the Eternal

Son;
Hail, Joseph, temple of the Eternal Spirit;
Hail, Joseph, beloved of the Trinity.
Hail, Joseph, spouse and companion of the Mother of God.
Hail, Joseph, friend of angels.
Hail, Joseph, believer in miracles.
Hail, Joseph, follower of dreams.
Hail, Joseph, lover of simplicity.
Hail, Joseph, exemplar of righteousness;
Hail, Joseph, model of meekness and patience;
Hail, Joseph, model of humility and obedience.
Blessed are the eyes that have seen what you saw.
Blessed are the ears that have heard what you heard.
Blessed are the arms that have embraced what you embraced.

Blessed is the lap that has held what you held.
Blessed is the heart that has loved what you loved.
Blessed is the Father who chose you;
Blessed is the Son who loved you:
Blessed is the Spirit who sanctified you.
Blessed is Mary, your spouse, who honoured and loved you.
Blessed is the angel who guarded and led you.
And blessed be forever all who remember and honour you. O Saint Joseph, faithful guardian,
guide our hearts in love,
keep us safe from harm,
and teach us trust and patience in God.
Amen.

— *Hail Joseph*

Day 8 — To God, Source of Wisdom and Peace

Father, guide my mind, steady my heart, and lead me closer to You.

Prayer

Gracious and holy Father,
grant us the intellect to understand you,
reason to discern you, diligence to seek you,
wisdom to find you, a spirit to know you,
a heart to meditate upon you.
May our ears hear you, may our eyes behold you,
and may our tongues proclaim you.
Give us grace that our way of life may be pleasing to you,
that we may have the patience to wait for you
and the perseverance to look for you.

Grant us a perfect end--your holy presence,
a blessed resurrection and life everlasting.
We ask this through Jesus Christ our Lord.

— *Prayer of St. Benedict*

Day 9 — To the Guardian Angel

My Guardian Angel,
guide me and keep me safe.

Prayer

Angel of God, my guardian dear,
to whom God's love commits me here,
ever be at my side,
to light and guard,
to rule and guide.
Amen.

— *Traditional Guardian Angel Prayer*

Day 10 — To Saint Patrick, Apostle of Ireland

Saint Patrick, faithful missionary and brave servant of God, fill my heart with courage to share God's love wherever I go.

Prayer

Christ with me, Christ before me, Christ behind me, Christ in me, Christ beneath me, Christ above me, Christ on my right, Christ on my left, Christ when I lie down, Christ when I sit down, Christ in the heart of every man who thinks of me, Christ in the mouth of every man who speaks of me, Christ in the eye that sees me, Christ in the ear that hears me.

I arise today.

Through a mighty strength, the invocation of the Trinity, through a belief in the Threeness, through a confession of the Oneness of the Creator of creation.

Amen.

— St. Patrick prayer

Day 11 — To Jesus, the Good Shepherd
Jesus, guide me and keep me close.

Prayer
O Good Shepherd,
lead me beside still waters,
restore my soul,
and keep me in Your love and
protection.
Amen.

— Psalm 23 & Good Shepherd Devotion (inspired)

Day 12 — To the Holy Spirit, Spirit of Strength

Holy Spirit, grant me courage and perseverance.

Prayer

Come, Holy Spirit,
Spirit of Strength,
fill my heart with fortitude,
guide my actions,
and help me trust God's plan.
Amen.

— Holy Spirit Devotion

Day 13 — To Jesus, Divine Mercy

Jesus, I trust in Your mercy.

Prayer

O Blood and Water,
which gushed forth from the Heart of Jesus,
forgive my sins,
restore my hope,

and fill me with Your endless mercy.
Amen.

— *Divine Mercy Prayer (St. Faustina)*

Day 14 — To Saint Michael the Archangel

Saint Michael, defend me from evil.

Prayer

Saint Michael the Archangel,

protect me from harm,

strengthen me to live in courage and faith,

and lead me in God's truth.

Amen.

— *Traditional St. Michael Prayer*

Day 15 — To Mary, Mother of Hope

Mother Mary, inspire hope in my heart.

Prayer

O Mary, Mother of Hope,

lift my heart from despair,

fill me with trust,
and lead me to Jesus' love.
Amen.

— *Marian Devotion*

Day 16 — To Jesus, Bread of Life

Jesus, nourish my soul with Your presence.

Prayer

O Jesus, Bread of Life,
feed my soul with Your grace,
fill my heart with love,
and unite me with Your sacred presence.
Amen.

— *Eucharistic Devotion (inspired)*

Day 17 — To the Holy Spirit, Spirit of Guidance

Holy Spirit, illuminate my mind and guide my decisions.

Prayer

Come, Holy Spirit,

Spirit of Guidance and Truth,

help me choose what is right,

strengthen my faith,

and lead me along God's path. Amen.

— *Holy Spirit Devotion*

Day 18 — To Saint Joseph, Worker and Protector

Saint Joseph, guide my work and protect my family.

Prayer

O Saint Joseph,

model of diligence and humility,

bless my work,

protect my loved ones,

and teach me to trust God in all things. Amen.

— *Litany of Saint Joseph (inspired)*

Day 19 — To Jesus, Light of the World

Jesus, shine in my heart and guide my way.

Prayer

O Jesus, Light of the World,

illuminate my soul,

show me Your truth,

and keep me close to Your love.

Amen.

— *Traditional Invocation to Christ the Light*

Day 20 — To Mary, Queen of Peace

Mother Mary, calm my heart and mind.

Prayer

O Queen of Peace,

soften my heart,

calm my thoughts,

and lead me closer to Jesus' love. Amen.

— *Regina Pacis Devotion*

Day 21 — To Jesus, Healer of the Sick

Jesus, heal my body, mind, and soul.

Prayer

Heavenly Father, I thank you for loving me. I thank you for sending your Son, Our Lord Jesus Christ, to the world to save and to set me free. I trust in your power and grace that sustain and restore me.

Loving Father, touch me now with your healing hands, for I believe that your will is for me to be well in mind, body, soul and spirit. Cover me with the most precious blood of your Son, our Lord, Jesus Christ from the top of my head to the soles of my feet.

— Healing Prayer

Day 22 — To the Holy Spirit, Spirit of Love

Holy Spirit, inflame my heart with Your love.

Prayer

Come, Holy Spirit,
Spirit of Love, burn away selfishness,
renew my faith, and draw me closer to God. Amen.

— Holy Spirit Devotion

Day 23 — To Mary, Mother of Consolation

Mother Mary, comfort me in my trials.

Prayer

O Mother of Consolation,
embrace me with your gentle care,
give me patience, courage, and hope,
and lead me to Jesus. Amen.

— Marian Devotion

Day 24 — To Jesus, the Good Shepherd

Jesus, guide me with Your gentle care.

Prayer

O Good Shepherd, lead me beside still waters, restore my soul,
and keep me in Your love. Amen.
Psalm 23 & Good Shepherd Devotion (inspired)

Day 25 — Prayer to St. Thomas Aquinas

St. Thomas, strengthen my faith and draw my heart closer to Jesus.

Prayer

Grant me, O Lord my God,
a mind to know you,
a heart to seek you,
wisdom to find you,
conduct pleasing to you,
faithful perseverance in waiting for you,

and a hope of finally embracing you.
Amen

— *Prayer to St. Thomas*

Day 26 — Prayer to the Sacred Heart of Jesus

Jesus, shape my heart to be gentle, humble, and obedient to Your will.

Prayer

O most holy heart of Jesus, fountain of every blessing, I adore you, I love you, and with lively sorrow for my sins, I offer you this poor heart of mine. Make me humble, patient, pure and wholly obedient to your will. Grant, good Jesus, that I may live in you and for you. Protect me in the midst of danger. Comfort me in my afflictions. Give me health of body, assistance in my temporal needs, your blessing on all that I do, and the grace of a holy death. Amen.

— *Prayer to scared Heart of Jesus*

Day 27 — To Jesus, Divine Mercy

Jesus, I trust in Your infinite mercy.

Prayer

O Blood and Water,
which gushed forth from the Heart of
Jesus, forgive my sins, renew my hope,
and fill me with Your mercy. Amen.

— *Divine Mercy Prayer (St. Faustina)*

Day 28 — To the Holy Spirit, Comforter of Souls

Holy Spirit, console me and bring peace to my heart.

Prayer

Come, Holy Spirit,
Comforter of Souls,
soothe my worries,

fill me with joy, and guide me in God's love. Amen.

— *Holy Spirit Devotion*

Day 29 — To Saint Joseph, Guardian of the Redeemer

Saint Joseph, protect my heart and home.

Prayer

O Saint Joseph,
guardian of Jesus and Mary,
watch over me and my family,
grant us safety, peace, and faith.
Amen.

— *Litany of Saint Joseph (inspired)*

Day 30 — To the God of Infinite Mercy

Lord, increase Your mercy in me and help me trust Your holy will.

Prayer

Eternal God,

in whom mercy is endless
and the treasury of compassion
inexhaustible, look kindly upon us and
increase Your mercy in us,
that in difficult moments we might not
despair nor become despondent,
but with great confidence submit
ourselves to Your holy will,
which is Love and Mercy itself. Amen.

Divine Mercy chaplet closing prayer

Day 31 — To Jesus, the Redeemer

Jesus, bless me with love and courage for a new month.

Prayer

O Jesus, Redeemer of the world,
strengthen my heart, renew my spirit,
and help me walk in Your mercy and love.
Amen.

AUGUST

Month of the Immaculate Heart of Mary

Affirmation for the Month

In this month of the Immaculate Heart of Mary, I open my heart to purity, love, and trust in God. Mother Mary, guide me with Your gentle care, protect my soul, and lead me closer to Jesus.

AUGUST

Day 1 — To Mary, Immaculate Heart

Mary, Mother of Love,
fill my heart with Your purity and grace.

Prayer

O Immaculate Heart of Mary,
teach me humility, patience, and
compassion. Help me love God with all
my heart and follow Jesus faithfully
each day. Amen.
— *Devotion to the Immaculate Heart of Mary*

Day 2 — To St. Jude, Helper in Times of Need

St. Jude, strengthen my heart and
remind me I am never alone.

Prayer

Most holy Apostle, St. Jude, friend of
Jesus, I place myself in your care at this
difficult time. Pray for me; help me
remember that I need not face my

troubles alone. Please join me in my need, asking God to send me consolation in my sorrow, courage in my fear, and healing in the midst of my suffering. Ask our loving God to fill me with the grace to accept whatever may lie ahead for me and my loved ones, and to strengthen my faith in God's healing power. Thank you, St. Jude, for the promise of hope you hold out to all who believe, and inspire me to give this gift of hope to others as it has been given to me. Amen.

St. Jude Prayer for Healing

Day 3 — To the Holy Spirit, Spirit of Peace

Holy Spirit, bring calm to my soul and mind.

Prayer

Come, Holy Spirit, Spirit of Peace,

quiet my heart, renew my hope,
and guide me in God's love and truth.
Amen.

— *Holy Spirit Devotion*

Day 4 — To Mary, Queen of Angels

Mother Mary,
protect me from all evil and harm.

Prayer

O Mary, Queen of Angels,
shield me from darkness and danger,
grant me courage to resist temptation,
and guide me safely in God's love.
Amen.

— *Marian Devotion (inspired)*

Day 5 — To Jesus, Victor over Evil

Jesus, Light of the World,
grant me victory over evil in my life.

Prayer

O Jesus, conqueror of sin and darkness,

protect me from evil thoughts and actions,
strengthen me in faith,
and help me walk in Your truth and light.
Amen.

— *Biblical Devotion*

Day 6 — To the Holy Spirit, Spirit of Guidance

Holy Spirit,
lead me in making good decisions.

Prayer

Come, Holy Spirit, Spirit of Guidance,
illuminate my mind and heart,
help me avoid mistakes,
and guide me toward what pleases God.
Amen.

— *Holy Spirit Devotion*

AUGUST

Day 7 — To Saint Joseph, Model of Obedience

Saint Joseph, teach me patience and trust in God's plan.

Prayer

O Saint Joseph, faithful servant of God,
help me follow God with patience,
obey His will in all things,
and face challenges with courage.
Amen.

— *Litany of Saint Joseph (inspired)*

Day 8 — To Mary, Mother of Hope

Mother Mary,
fill me with hope and courage.

Prayer

O Mary,
Mother of Hope,
lift my heart from fear and despair,
strengthen me to trust God's timing,

and open my life to new opportunities.
Amen.

— *Marian Devotion*

Day 9 — To Saint Blaise, Protector of Health

Saint Blaise, intercede for me.
Protect me from every illness of body
and spirit, and keep me strong in faith.

Prayer

O Blessed Saint Blaise,
hear my prayer.
Grant me health of throat and body,
and protect me from all harm. Through
your intercession, may I always praise
God with a grateful heart. Amen.

— *Saint Blaise prayer*

Day 10 — To the Guardian Angel

My Guardian Angel,
guide me in new beginnings.

Prayer

Angel of God, my guardian dear,
show me the right path,
protect me from harm,
and help me embrace God's
opportunities with courage.
Amen.

— *Traditional Guardian Angel Prayer*

Day 11 — To Jesus, Healer of the Broken-hearted

Jesus, my healer and comforter.
Heal my wounds, restore my peace, and renew my faith.

Prayer

O Jesus, Divine Physician, touch my heart and heal my body and spirit. Grant me patience and faith in Your loving will. Amen.

— *Healing Prayer*

Day 12 — To the Precious Blood of Jesus

Jesus, Your blood redeems and protects.
Wash me clean and make my heart
new.

Prayer

By the Precious Blood of Jesus, deliver
me from evil and protect my soul.
May I live in purity and grace.
Amen.

— Devotion to the Precious Blood

Day 13 — To the Holy Spirit, Spirit of Courage

Holy Spirit,
ignite courage in my heart to do what
is right.

Prayer

Come, Holy Spirit, Spirit of Courage,
strengthen my faith,
help me resist temptation,

and guide me in all righteous choices.
Amen.

— *Holy Spirit Devotion*

Day 14 — To Saint Michael the Archangel

Saint Michael, protect me from evil and danger.

Prayer

Saint Michael the Archangel,
defend me in battle,
protect me from all evil,
and grant me courage to follow God's will.
Amen.

— *Traditional St. Michael Prayer*

Day 15 — To Mary, Mother of Consolation

Mother Mary,
comfort me in trials and uncertainty.

Prayer

O Mother of Consolation, soothe my worries, grant me patience and trust, and lead me to Jesus' love. Amen.

— *Marian Devotion*

Day 16 — To Saint Francis de Sales, Patron of Gentle Hearts

Saint Francis, teach me gentleness and patience. Help me live each day with kindness, calmness, and trust in God's mercy.

Prayer

O Saint Francis de Sales, gentle and wise teacher of God's love, intercede for me that I may grow in patience, gentleness, and charity in all my actions. Amen.

— *Traditional Prayer to Saint Francis de Sales*

AUGUST

Day 17 — To the Holy Spirit, Spirit of Wisdom

Holy Spirit,
help me discern right from wrong.

Prayer

Come, Holy Spirit, Spirit of Wisdom,
guide my choices,
protect me from bad decisions,
and teach me obedience and patience.
Amen.

— *Veni Sancte Spiritus (inspired)*

Day 18 — To Christ, My Refuge and Strength

Jesus, draw me close and keep me in
Your loving protection.

Prayer

Soul of Christ, sanctify me,
Body of Christ, save me,
Blood of Christ, inebriate me,
Water from the side of Christ, wash me,

Passion of Christ, strengthen me,
O good Jesus, hear me.
Hide me within your wounds,
keep me close to you,
defend me from the evil enemy,
call me at the hour of my death,
and bid me to come to you,
to praise you with your saints,
forever and ever. Amen.

— *Anima Christi*

Day 19 — To God Our Father

God, my loving Father, You watch over me. I rest in Your care, trusting Your mercy and love to surround me.

Prayer

Watch, O Lord, with those who wake, or watch, or weep, and give Your angels charge over those who sleep.
Tend to Your sick ones, O Lord Christ; rest Your weary ones; bless Your dying

ones; soothe Your suffering ones; pity Your afflicted ones; shield Your joyous ones; and all for Your love's sake.
Amen.

— *St. Augustine's Evening Prayer*

Day 20 — To the Blessed Virgin Mary, Mother of God

Holy Mother Mary, you are my gentle guide. Guide me, hold me close, and lead me safely to your Son.

Prayer

Remember, O most gracious Virgin Mary, that never was it known
that anyone who fled to your protection, implored your help,
or sought your intercession,
was left unaided.
Inspired with this confidence,
I fly to you, O Virgin of virgins, my Mother.

To you I come, before you I stand,
sinful and sorrowful.
O Mother of the Word Incarnate,
despise not my petitions,
but in your mercy hear and answer me.
Amen.

— *The Memorare (Traditional Marian Prayer)*

Day 21 — To the Guardian Angel

Guardian Angel,
guide me in patience and good decisions.

Prayer

Angel of God, my guardian dear,
light my path,
help me choose wisely,
and keep me safe from harm.
Amen.

— *Traditional Guardian Angel Prayer*

Day 22 — To Saint Agnes, Pure and Faithful

Saint Agnes, model of purity and courage, help me remain faithful to God in all I do and guard my heart with love and devotion.

Prayer

St. Agnes, although you were only a child, you believed that Jesus was always with you; help us to remember that he is also with us, and to remain true to his presence.

St. Agnes, you refused to give up your faith; help us to be proud of our faith, to love it, to be strong in it, and to give witness to it daily.

St. Agnes, patron saint of children, watch over the children of the world; keep them safe from harm; be with them in their hour of need; and always pray for them. Amen.

— *Traditional Prayer to Saint Agnes*

Day 23 — To Jesus, Victor over Evil

Jesus, protect me from sin and darkness.

Prayer

O Jesus, conqueror of evil, shield me from temptation, renew my courage, and guide me in all righteousness. Amen.

— *Biblical Devotion*

Day 24 — To the Holy Spirit, Spirit of Hope

Holy Spirit, fill me with hope and new opportunities.

Prayer

Come, Holy Spirit, Spirit of Hope, open my heart to God's blessings,

guide me in patience and courage,
and lead me to new beginnings. Amen.

— *Holy Spirit Devotion*

Day 25 — To the Holy Spirit, Consoler of Hearts

Holy Spirit, bring comfort and understanding. Guide my decisions, inspire my prayers, and fill me with faith and peace.

Prayer

Come, Holy Spirit,
give me wisdom, understanding,
counsel, fortitude, knowledge, piety,
and fear of the Lord.
Let Your gifts guide me in all I do.
Amen.

— *Traditional Gifts of the Holy Spirit Prayer*

Day 26 — To Saint Joseph, Terror of Demons

Saint Joseph, strong protector.
Defend me from evil, protect my home, and guide me in faith.

Prayer

O Saint Joseph, Terror of Demons,
stand between me and all spiritual harm.
Guide my steps and lead me to safety in God's love.
Amen.

— Traditional Prayer to Saint Joseph

Day 27 — To Mother Mary, Queen of Angels

Holy Mother Mary, watch over me.
Lead me with your angels' guidance and draw me closer to Your Son.

Prayer

Hail Mary, full of grace,

the Lord is with thee;
blessed art thou among women,
and blessed is the fruit of thy womb,
Jesus.
Holy Mary, Mother of God,
pray for us sinners, now and at the hour
of our death.
Amen.

— *Traditional Hail Mary*

Day 28 — To the Holy Spirit, Spirit of Courage

Holy Spirit, ignite boldness in my heart.

Prayer

Come, Holy Spirit, Spirit of Courage,
strengthen my faith,
help me face challenges with trust,
and guide me in God's plan.
Amen.

— *Holy Spirit Devotion*

Day 29 — To Mary, Mother of Perpetual Help

Mother Mary, guide me in my struggles and decisions.

Prayer

O Mary, Mother of Perpetual Help,
teach me patience and obedience,
fill me with hope and courage,
and lead me to Jesus' love. Amen.

— *Marian Devotion*

Day 30 — To the Blessed Virgin Mary, Our Lady of Lourdes

Mother Mary, healer of the sick, you comfort those who suffer. Intercede for us and bring us healing and peace.

Prayer

O ever-Immaculate Virgin,
Mother of Mercy, Health of the Sick,
Refuge of Sinners,
comfort me in my sorrows and obtain

for me healing,

according to Your Son's will.

Amen.

— *Prayer to Our Lady of Lourdes*

Day 31 — To Saint George, Defender of Faith

Saint George, brave soldier of Christ.

Grant me courage to face all trials and stand strong in faith.

Prayer

Saint George, warrior of God,

protect me from all evil and harm.

Give me strength to fight temptation

and remain faithful to Christ's love.

Amen.

— *Traditional Prayer to Saint George*

SEPTEMBER

Month of Our Lady of Sorrows

Affirmation for the Month

In this month of Our Lady of Sorrows,
I open my heart to compassion,
patience, and courage.
Mother Mary, guide me through life's
trials, teach me to trust in God,
and lead me closer to Your Son, Jesus.

SEPTEMBER

Day 1 — To Mary, Mother of Sorrows

Mother Mary, comfort me in my trials and pain.

Prayer

O Mother of Sorrows, stand with me in moments of grief and worry. Teach me patience and hope, and guide me to the loving heart of Jesus. Amen.

— *Marian Devotion*

Day 2 — To Jesus, Comforter in Suffering

Jesus, my refuge, be my strength in times of sorrow.

Prayer

O Jesus, Comforter of the afflicted, heal my wounds, give me courage to face difficulties, and fill my heart with hope and peace. Amen.

— *Biblical Devotion*

Day 3 — Prayer to the Sacred Heart of Jesus

Jesus Christ, grant me endurance and perseverance.

Prayer

Heart of Jesus, aflame with love for us, Have Mercy on us. Heart of Jesus, Source of justice and love, Have Mercy on us. Heart of Jesus, treasure house of wisdom and knowledge, Have Mercy on us. Heart of Jesus, In whom there dwells the fullness of God, Have Mercy on us. Jesus, gentle and humble of heart, Touch our hearts and make them like your own. We make this prayer to You and to your Father and the Holy Spirit Who live and reign forever and ever. Amen.

— Prayer to the sacred Heart of Jesus

Day 4 — To St. Joseph, Strong Protector

St. Joseph, guard my life and guide my heart with your gentle strength.

Prayer

Oh, St. Joseph, whose protection is so great, so prompt, so strong, before the throne of God, I place in you all my interests and desires.

Oh, St. Joseph, do assist me by your powerful intercession, and obtain for me from your Divine Son all spiritual blessings, through Jesus Christ, our Lord. So that, having engaged here below your heavenly power, I may offer my thanksgiving and homage to the most loving of fathers.

Oh, St. Joseph, I never weary contemplating you and Jesus asleep in your arms; I dare not approach while he

reposes near your heart.
Press him in my name and kiss his fine head for me and ask him to return the kiss when I draw my dying breath.

St. Joseph, patron of departing souls - pray for me.
Amen.

— *Saint Joseph's prayer*

Day 5 — To Mary, Mother of Consolation

Mother Mary, comfort me in sorrow and trials.

Prayer

O Mother of Consolation, soothe my worries, fill my heart with hope,
and lead me to Jesus' love and peace.
Amen.

— *Marian Devotion*

Day 6 — To Jesus, Divine Healer

Jesus, heal my heart and soul.

Prayer

O Jesus, Divine Healer, forgive my sins, restore my spirit, and fill me with love, courage, and hope.
Amen.

— *Healing Prayer (inspired)*

Day 7 — To the Holy Spirit, Spirit of Guidance

Holy Spirit, help me make good choices and avoid bad decisions.

Prayer

Come, Holy Spirit, Spirit of Guidance, illuminate my mind and heart, lead me to what pleases God, and teach me patience and obedience.
Amen.

— *Holy Spirit Devotion*

Day 8 — Celebrating the Nativity Feast of Mary

Mary, born to bring God's light, guide me in love and humility.

Prayer

O Mary, whose Nativity Feast brought hope to the world, help me live with purity and obedience, fill my heart with courage and faith, and lead me to Jesus.
Amen.

— *Marian Devotion (Nativity Feast of Mary)*

Day 9 — To Our Father in Heaven

Father, guide my steps and help me trust Your loving will.

Prayer

Our Father, Who art in heaven, Hallowed be Thy Name. Thy Kingdom come.

Thy Will be done,
on earth as it is in Heaven.

Give us this day our daily bread.
And forgive us our trespasses,
as we forgive those who trespass
against us. Lead us not into
temptation, but deliver us from evil.
Amen.

— *The Lord's Prayer*

Day 10 — To Saint Patrick, Apostle of Ireland

Saint Patrick, faithful missionary and brave servant of God, fill my heart with courage to share God's love wherever I go.

Prayer

Christ with me, Christ before me, Christ behind me, Christ in me, Christ beneath me, Christ above me, Christ on my right, Christ on my left, Christ when I lie down, Christ when I sit down, Christ in the heart of every man who thinks of me, Christ in the mouth of every man who speaks of me,

Christ in the eye that sees me, Christ in the ear that hears me.

I arise today.

Through a mighty strength, the invocation of the Trinity,

Through a belief in the Threeness,
Through a confession of the Oneness
Of the Creator of creation.
Amen.

— *St. Patrick prayer*

Day 11 — To God, My Eternal Father
Father, draw me closer to Your heart and teach me to love as You love.

Prayer

Almighty God, my Eternal Father, from the fullness of my soul I adore You. I am deeply grateful that You have made me in Your image and likeness, and that You ever hold me in Your loving embrace. Direct me to love You with all my heart, with all my soul, and with my whole mind. Direct me to love all Your children as I love myself. O, my Father, my soul longs to be united to You, and to rest in You forever. Have the Holy Spirit touch my soul so that I may love You as He does, and as Your Beloved Son Jesus does. Amen

— *Prayer to Heavenly Father*

Day 12 — To the Holy Spirit, Spirit of Hope

Holy Spirit, fill me with hope and courage.

Prayer

Come, Holy Spirit, Spirit of Hope,
open my heart to God's blessings,
strengthen me in patience,
and guide me toward new
opportunities. Amen.

— *Holy Spirit Devotion*

Day 13 — To Jesus, the Good Shepherd

Jesus, my Good Shepherd, Lead me gently today. When I am confused, guide me. When I am afraid, comfort me. When I am weak, strengthen me.

Prayer

Lord Jesus, Good Shepherd who never abandons His flock, walk with me through this day. Hold me close to Your Heart and lead me along the path of peace. Amen.

— *Traditional Devotion to the Good Shepherd*

Day 14 — To God, My Companion in Every Moment

Lord, be with me in all I do today. Guide my thoughts, bless my work, and keep my heart at peace.

Prayer

Heavenly Father, as I begin this day, fill my workplace with Your peace and order. Guide my decisions, bless my efforts, and strengthen me when I grow weary. May my words and actions reflect Your love to everyone I meet. Watch over my home and my family, and keep me safe in all my comings and goings. Thank You for Your constant care. In Jesus' name, Amen.

— *Prayer before work (Inspired)*

Day 15 — To St. Jude, Bearer of Hope in Hard Times

St. Jude, stand with me in my struggles and strengthen my heart with hope.

Prayer

Most holy Apostle, St. Jude, friend of Jesus, I place myself in your care at this difficult time. Pray for me; help me remember that I need not face my troubles alone. Please join me in my need, asking God to send me consolation in my sorrow, courage in my fear, and healing in the midst of my suffering. Ask our loving God to fill me with the grace to accept whatever may lie ahead for me and my loved ones, and to strengthen my faith in God's healing power. Thank you, St. Jude, for the promise of hope you hold out to all who believe, and inspire me to give this gift of hope to others as it has been given to me. Amen.

— *St Jude Prayer*

Day 16 — To Saint Gabriel the Archangel

Saint Gabriel, messenger of God.
Help me listen for God's voice
and say yes with courage and joy.

Prayer

Saint Gabriel, holy messenger of the Lord, open my ears to God's whisper and guide me in doing His will with faith and humility. Amen.

— *Traditional Gabriel devotion (inspired)*

Day 17 — To Saint George, Courageous Martyr

Saint George, brave witness of Christ.
Strengthen me in faith and help me
resist the enemy's attacks.

Prayer

O Saint George,
victorious soldier of Christ,
defend me from all evil
and give me courage
to stand firm in God's truth.
Amen.

— Traditional St. George devotion (inspired)

Day 18 — To Mother Mary, Destroyer of the Devil

Blessed Virgin Mary, mighty defender. Crush the enemy beneath your feet and protect my soul with your light.

Prayer

O Mary, Immaculate Conqueror, destroyer of the devil, guard me with your mantle of grace, and lead me safely to your Son. Amen.

— Traditional Marian Invocation

SEPTEMBER

Day 19 — To Jesus, Healer of the Heart

Jesus, heal my soul and grant me hope.

Prayer

O Jesus, Divine Healer, restore my
spirit, fill my heart with love,
and strengthen me to face life with
courage. Amen.

— *Healing Prayer (inspired)*

Day 20 — To the Holy Spirit, Giver of Every Good Fruit

Holy Spirit, fill my heart and shape my life with Your love and grace.

Prayer

Come, Holy Spirit, fill my heart with Your presence and love. Grant me the fruits of Your Spirit:
love to care for others sincerely,
joy to rejoice in Your blessings,
peace to calm my heart in every moment, **patience** to endure trials with

grace, **kindness** to serve others with compassion, **goodness** to choose what is holy and true, **faithfulness** to remain steadfast in Your ways, **gentleness** to act with humility, and **self-control** to follow God's will.

Holy Spirit, guide me each day, that my life may reflect Your love and goodness. Come, Holy Spirit, Spirit of Strength, guide me in challenges, help me trust God's plan, and fill my heart with hope. Amen.

— *Prayer for the Fruits of the Holy Spirit*

Day 21 — To Mary, Mother of Consolation

Mother Mary, comfort me in times of sorrow.

Prayer

O Mother of Consolation,

soothe my heart, give me patience and faith, and lead me to Jesus' love. Amen.

— *Marian Devotion*

Day 22 — To Jesus, Bread of Life
Jesus, nourish my soul and strengthen my spirit.

Prayer
O Jesus, Bread of Life, feed my heart with Your grace, fill me with courage and love, and guide me in Your holy ways. Amen.

— *Eucharistic Devotion*

Day 23 — To St. John Bosco
St. John Bosco, guide the young in faith and love.

Prayer
O St. John Bosco, protector of children and youth, help me guide the young with patience and wisdom, fill my heart

with courage, hope, and joy, and lead all souls closer to God's love. Amen.

Prayer to St. John Bosco

Day 24 — To Divine Mercy

Jesus, Your mercy restores and heals.

Prayer

O Divine Mercy of Jesus, pour Your loving kindness upon the world, heal the broken-hearted, protect the innocent, and fill our hearts with courage, hope, and faith. You expired, Jesus, but the source of life gushed forth for souls, and the ocean of mercy opened up for the whole world. O Fount of Life, unfathomable Divine Mercy, envelop the whole world and empty Yourself out upon us. Amen.

— *Divine Mercy Prayer Inspired*

Day 25 — To St. Clare of Assisi

St. Clare, teach me simplicity and devotion.

Prayer

O St. Clare, humble servant of God, help me walk with simplicity and love, strengthen my heart with patience and hope, and guide my actions in faith and devotion. Amen.

— *Prayer St. Clare of Assisi*

Day 26 — To the Holy Spirit, giver of light and life.

Holy Spirit, fill me with wisdom and guidance.

Prayer

Come, Holy Spirit, illuminate my mind and guide my steps, grant me courage, patience, and understanding, and lead me closer to God's perfect will. Amen.

Day 27 — To St. Lucy

St. Lucy, shine light upon my path.

Prayer

O St. Lucy, beacon of God's light,
illuminate my thoughts and heart with
hope, protect my family and loved ones,
and fill my life with faith, courage, and
joy. Amen.

— *Prayer to St. Lucy*

Day 28 — To Mary, Undoer of Knots

Mother Mary, help me untangle my
difficulties.

Prayer

O Mary, Undoer of Knots,
bring clarity to my decisions,
restore peace in my heart,
and guide me to Jesus' guidance. Amen.

— *Mary Undoer of Knots Devotion*

Day 28 — To Mary, Mother of All Children

Mother Mary, protect the little ones.

Prayer

O Mary, Mother of All Children, watch over every child with Your loving care, keep them safe from harm, and guide their hearts to grow in faith, hope, and love. Amen.

— *Marian Devotion*

Day 29 — To the Infant Jesus

Infant Jesus, bring innocence, joy, and peace.

Prayer

O Infant Jesus, fill my heart with childlike faith and purity, renew my spirit with joy and gentleness, and bless my home with peace and love. Amen.

— *Infant Jesus Prayer inspired*

Day 30 — To St. Stephen the Martyr

St. Stephen, inspire courage and forgiveness.

Prayer

O St. Stephen, first martyr of Christ, teach me to forgive with a peaceful heart, grant me courage to choose what is right, and fill my soul with compassion and faith. Amen.

— *Prayer to St. Stephen the Marty*

OCTOBER

Month of the Holy Rosary

Affirmation for the Month

In this month of the Holy Rosary,
I open my heart to prayer, reflection,
and trust. Mary, Mother of the Rosary,
guide my thoughts, strengthen my
faith, and lead me closer to Jesus
through each mystery.

Day 1 — To Mary, Seat of Wisdom

Mary, guide my thoughts with clarity and peace.

Prayer

O Mary, Seat of Wisdom, enlighten my mind with understanding, help me choose what is good and pleasing to God, and fill my heart with patience, faith, and hope. Amen

— *Marian Devotion*

Day 2 — To the Eucharistic Lord

Jesus present in the Eucharist, nourish my soul.

Prayer

O Jesus in the Blessed Sacrament, fill my heart with Your healing presence, renew my strength in moments of weakness, and guide me in love, humility, and faith. O my God, I love you above all things, with my whole heart and soul, because You are all good and worthy of all love. I love my neighbour as myself for the love of You. I forgive all who have injured me, and ask pardon of all whom I have injured. Amen

— *Eucharist Devotion*

Day 3 — To St. John the Apostle

St. John, teach me to love with a faithful heart.

Prayer

O St. John, beloved disciple,
help me love others with truth and compassion, grant me a heart full of peace and courage, and guide me closer to the light of Christ. Amen.

— *Prayer to St. John the Apostle*

Day 4 — Prayer To St. Benedict

St. Benedict, guard us against temptation.

Prayer

O St. Benedict, holy protector, shield me from harm and temptation, strengthen my spirit with discipline and peace, and guide me safely along God's holy path. Amen.

— *Prayer to St. Benedict*

Day 5 — To Divine Hope

Lord, fill my heart with unwavering hope.

Prayer

O Jesus, source of eternal hope,
lift my heart when I am weary,
fill me with courage to trust in Your timing, and guide me in faith, patience, and love. Amen.

Day 6— To St. Anthony of Padua

St. Anthony, helper in need. Come to our aid when we most need you and intercede for us.

Prayer

O St. Anthony, gentle wonder-worker, bring peace to troubled hearts, guide me in times of confusion and worry, and fill my life with clarity, trust, and hope. Amen.

— *Prayer to St. Anthony of Padua*

Day 7 — To the Holy Spirit, Spirit of Strength

Holy Spirit, be my refuge and my courage.

Prayer

Come, Holy Spirit, strengthen me in every trial, fill me with wisdom, calm, and courage, and lead me to walk

faithfully in God's love.
Amen.

— *Holy spirit Devotion*

Day 8 — To St. Andrew the Apostle

St. Andrew, inspire courage in following Christ.

Prayer

O St. Andrew, devoted follower of Jesus, guide me to answer God's call with courage, fill my heart with steadfast faith and hope, and help me serve others with love and humility. Amen.

— *Prayer to St. Andrew*

Day 9 — To St. Raphael the Archangel

St. Raphael, bearer of healing and peace. Pray for me that my mind is at rest and I am filled with Lord's spirit.

Prayer

O St. Raphael, gentle healer, bring God's

peace into my heart and home, guide me toward strength, wholeness, and hope, and protect me on every path I walk. Amen.

Prayer to St. Raphael the Archangel

Day 10— To the Holy Spirit, Giver of New Beginnings

Holy Spirit, renew my heart and my life.

Prayer

Come, Holy Spirit of Renewal, refresh my thoughts with clarity and peace, open doors to new opportunities and grace, and lead me forward with courage and joy. Amen.

— *Hopy Spirit Devotion*

Day 11 — To St. Faustina

St. Faustina, witness of Divine Mercy, guide my heart in trust.

Prayer

O St. Faustina, teach me to trust in Jesus with a simple and humble heart, help me surrender my worries to His mercy, and fill my soul with hope, peace, and compassion for others. Amen.

— *Prayer to St. Faustina*

Day 12 — To Jesus, Light of the Nations

Jesus, shine Your peace upon the world.

Prayer

O Jesus, Light of the Nations, fill the world with peace and healing, brighten my heart with hope and trust, and guide me to walk in Your love each day. Amen.

— *Prayer for Peace and Guidance*

Day 13— To the Infant Jesus
Infant Jesus, bring innocence, joy, and peace.

Prayer
O Infant Jesus, fill my heart with childlike faith and purity, renew my spirit with joy and gentleness, and bless my home with peace and love. Amen.

— *Infant Jesus Prayer inspired*

Day 14 — To St. Stephen the Martyr
St. Stephen, inspire courage and forgiveness.

Prayer
O St. Stephen, first martyr of Christ, teach me to forgive with a peaceful heart, grant me courage to choose what is right, and fill my soul with compassion and faith. Amen.

— *Prayer to St. Stephen the Martyr*

Day 15 — To St. John the Baptist

St. John, prepare my heart for the Lord.

Prayer

O St. John the Baptist, guide me to turn away from fear and doubt, prepare my heart for God's grace and mercy, and strengthen me to live with courage and hope.
Amen.

— *Prayer to St. John the Baptist*

Day 16 — To the Holy Family

Jesus, Mary, and Joseph, bless and protect families.

Prayer

O Holy Family of Nazareth, watch over my home with love and peace, grant unity, patience, and courage to all families, and guide us to live in faith and kindness. Amen
— *Prayer to the Holy Family*

Day 17 — To St. Bridget of Sweden

St. Bridget, guide me in prayer and strengthen my heart in times of difficulty.

Prayer

O St. Bridget of Sweden,
teach me to pray with sincerity and trust, help me remain strong in trials and hardship, and fill my heart with hope, courage, and peace. Amen.

— *Prayer to St. Bridget of Sweden*

Day 18 — To the Holy Spirit, Spirit of Protection

Holy Spirit, guard my mind, heart, and home.

Prayer

Come, Holy Spirit of Protection, shield me from despair and temptation, fill my heart with courage, clarity, and peace, and guide me safely into God's loving will. Amen.

— *Holy Spirit Devotion*

Day 19 — To Mary, Help of Christians

Mary, protector of all,
watch over my family and friends.

Prayer

O Mary, Help of Christians,
protect my loved ones from harm,
guide our hearts in love and faith,
and surround us with Your motherly care.
Amen.

— *Marian Devotion*

Day 20 — To the Holy Spirit, Spirit of Joy

Holy Spirit, fill me with Your presence.

Prayer

Come, Holy Spirit, Spirit of Joy and Life,

fill my heart with Your gifts, guide me in using my talents for good, and lead me closer to God each day.
Amen.

— *Holy Spirit Devotion*

Day 21 — To Mary, Mother of All Children

Mother Mary, protect the little ones.

Prayer

O Mary, Mother of All Children,
watch over every child with Your loving care, keep them safe from harm, and guide their hearts to grow in faith, hope, and love. Amen.

— *Marian Devotion*

Day 22 — To Jesus, King of Glory

Jesus, fill me with hope and courage.

Prayer

O Jesus, King of Glory,

strengthen my heart in trials,
fill me with hope for new beginnings,
and help me trust Your plan for my life.
Amen.

— *Biblical Devotion (inspired)*

Day 26 — To Mary, Queen of the Holy Rosary

Mary, guide my prayer and devotion.

Prayer

O Queen of the Holy Rosary,
teach me to meditate on Jesus' life,
protect my loved ones, and fill my heart with courage, hope, and love.
Amen.

— *Marian Devotion*

Day 27 — To Jesus, Shepherd of Souls

Jesus, lead me in love and protection.

Prayer

O Jesus, Shepherd of Souls,

guide my heart in faith and obedience,
protect my family and friends,
and fill me with courage, hope, and joy.
Amen.

— *Inspired by Biblical Devotion*

Day 28 — Anima Christi
Soul of Christ, come and dwell within me; guide and protect me always.

Prayer
Soul of Christ, sanctify me.
Body of Christ, save me.
Blood of Christ, inebriate me.
Water from the side of Christ, wash me.
Passion of Christ, strengthen me.
O good Jesus, hear me.
Within Thy wounds, hide me.
Separated from Thee let me never be.
From the malignant enemy, defend me.
At the hour of death, call me.
To come to Thee, bid me,

That I may praise Thee in the company
Of Thy Saints, for all eternity. Amen.

— *Anima Christi*

Day 29 — To Saint Patrick, Apostle of Ireland

Saint Patrick, faithful missionary and brave servant of God.
Fill my heart with courage
to share God's love wherever I go.

Prayer

Christ with me, Christ before me, Christ behind me, Christ in me, Christ beneath me, Christ above me, Christ on my right, Christ on my left, Christ when I lie down, Christ when I sit down, Christ in the heart of every man who thinks of me, Christ in the mouth of every man who speaks of me,

Christ in the eye that sees me, Christ in the ear that hears me.

I arise today.

Through a mighty strength, the invocation of the Trinity,

Through a belief in the Threeness,

Through a confession of the Oneness

Of the Creator of creation. Amen.

— *St. Patrick prayer*

Day 30— To St. Francis of Assisi

St. Francis, teach me simplicity, love, and peace.

Prayer

O St. Francis, gentle servant of God,
help me live with humility and joy,
protect the children and the poor,
and guide my heart in courage, hope,
and love.
Amen.

— *Saint Prayer (inspired)*

Day 31 — To St. John the Baptist

St. John, prepare my heart for the Lord.

Prayer

O St. John the Baptist, guide me to turn away from fear and doubt, prepare my heart for God's grace and mercy, and strengthen me to live with courage and hope. Amen.

— Prayer to St. John the Baptist

NOVEMBER

Month of the Departed

Affirmation for the Month

In this month of the Holy Souls,
I remember those who have gone before
me, trusting in God's mercy and love.
I pray for the faithful departed,
and open my heart to forgiveness, hope,
and courage.

Day 1 — To our Father, prayer for eternal rest.

Lord, have mercy on all souls.

Prayer

In your hands, O Lord, we humbly entrust our brothers and sisters. In this life you embraced them with your tender love; deliver them now from every evil and bid them eternal rest. The old order has passed away: welcome them into paradise, where there will be no sorrow, no weeping or pain, but the fullness of peace and joy with your Son and the Holy Spirit forever and ever. Amen.

— *Prayer for eternal rest*

Day 2 — To Mary, Mother of the Faithful

Mother Mary, pray for the souls in your care.

Prayer
O Mary, Mother of the Faithful, intercede for all who have gone before us, comfort the grieving, and lead us closer to Jesus with hope and courage.
Amen.

— *Marian intercession for the souls*

Day 3 — To the Holy Spirit, Spirit of Healing

Holy Spirit, heal hearts touched by loss.

Prayer
Come, Holy Spirit, Spirit of Healing, fill my heart with peace and hope, comfort those who mourn, and guide my thoughts toward God's mercy and love.
Amen.

— *Holy Spirit Devotion*

Day 4 — To Saint Michael the Archangel

Saint Michael, defend the souls and the living.

Prayer

Saint Michael, mighty protector,
shield the souls of the faithful departed,
guard me, my family, and children from harm,
and strengthen us with courage and hope.
Amen.

— *Inspired St. Michael Prayer*

Day 5 — To Mary, Queen of Souls

Mary, intercede for the faithful departed.

Prayer

O Mary, Queen of Souls,
bring light to those in purgatory,
grant peace to the grieving,

and fill our hearts with patience, hope, and love.
Amen.

— *Marian Devotion*

Day 6 — To Heavenly Father, Divine Healer

Heavenly Father, Divine Healer,
restore my soul and spirit.

Prayer

Loving Father, touch me now with your healing hands, for I believe that your will is for me to be well in mind, body, soul and spirit. Cover me with the most precious blood of your Son, our Lord, Jesus Christ from the top of my head to the soles of my feet. Amen

— *From the Prayer attributed to St. Padre Pio*

Day 7 — To the Guardian Angel

My Guardian Angel, protect and guide me.

Prayer

Angel of God, my faithful guide, watch over my family, friends, and children, keep us safe from harm and temptation, and lead our hearts to Jesus in hope and love. Amen.

— *Traditional Devotion*

Day 8 — To Mary, Mother of Hope

Mother Mary, bring light to sorrowful hearts.

Prayer

O Mary, Mother of Hope, comfort those who mourn, grant courage to the living, and lead all souls to eternal peace in Jesus. Amen.

— *Marian Devotion*

NOVEMBER

Day 9 — To Jesus, Divine Protector

Jesus, protect my family and friends.

Prayer

O Jesus, Divine Protector,
shield us from harm and evil,
strengthen our hearts with faith and
patience, and guide our talents and
actions for Your glory.
Amen.

— *Devotion Inspired by Scripture*

Day 10 — To the Holy Spirit, Spirit of Hope

Holy Spirit, fill us with light, courage, and joy.

Prayer

Come, Holy Spirit, fill the hearts of your faithful and kindle in them the fire of your love. Send forth your Spirit and they shall be created, and you shall renew the face of the earth.

O God, who have taught the hearts of the faithful by the light of the Holy Spirit, grant that in the same Spirit we may be truly wise and ever rejoice in his consolation through Christ our Lord. Amen.

— *Holy Spirit Prayer*

Day 11 — To Saint Joseph, Protector of Families

Saint Joseph, guide and protect my loved ones.

Prayer

O Saint Joseph, faithful guardian,
watch over my family and friends,
grant us courage, patience, and trust,
and lead us closer to Jesus in all things.
Amen.

— *Litany of Saint Joseph (inspired)*

NOVEMBER

Day 12 — To St. Jude, Patron of Hope

St. Jude, bring hope to hearts in despair.

Prayer

O St. Jude, faithful intercessor,
pray for those who feel lost or hopeless,
fill our hearts with courage and
perseverance, and guide us to Jesus'
mercy and love. Amen.

— *Saint Jude Prayer*

Day 13 — To Mary, Mother of Mercy

Mother Mary, comfort hearts in sorrow.

Prayer

O Mary, Mother of Mercy,
embrace the faithful departed with Your
love, bring peace to those who mourn,
and guide our hearts to hope, patience,
and joy. Amen.

— *Marian Devotion*

Day 14 — To St. Anthony of Padua
St. Anthony, guide me to find God's wisdom.

Prayer
St. Anthony, helper in need.
Guide me to find God's wisdom.

Prayer
I salute you, St. Anthony, lily of purity, ornament and glory of Christianity.

I salute you, great Saint, cherub of wisdom and seraph of divine love. I rejoice at the favours Our Lord has so liberally bestowed on you.

In humility and confidence, I entreat you to help me, for I know that God has given you charity and compassion, as well as power.

I ask you, by the love you felt toward the Holy Infant Jesus as you held Him in your arms, to tell Him now of the favours I seek through your intercession. *(Mention your petition.)*

O glorious favourite of God, in humble reverence I petition you to grant me what I so urgently ask for, and I will make known your goodness and holiness, thereby to honour and glorify Him who has so greatly blessed you. Amen.

O St. Anthony, gentle wonder-worker, bring peace to troubled hearts,
guide me in times of confusion and worry, and fill my life with clarity, trust, and hope.
Amen.

— *Prayer to St. Anthony in any necessity*

Day 15 — To Jesus, Divine Protector
Jesus, shield my heart, family, and friends.

Prayer

O Jesus, Divine Protector,
guard us from harm and temptation,
strengthen our hearts with hope and faith, and lead us in love, patience, and courage.
Amen.

— *Prayer to Divine Protector*

Day 16 — To the Holy Spirit, Spirit of Guidance

Holy Spirit, fill my heart with wisdom.

Prayer

Come, Holy Spirit, Spirit of Guidance,
lead my thoughts, words, and actions,
help me use my gifts for good,
and strengthen me in hope, patience, and courage. Amen.

— *Holy Spirit Devotion*

NOVEMBER

Day 17 — To St. Therese of Lisieux

St. Therese, help me trust God in small deeds.

Prayer

O St. Therese, little flower of love, teach me to do small acts with great faith, fill my heart with hope, joy, and courage, and guide me to serve God and others with love. Amen.

— *Prayer St. Therese of Lisieu*

Day 18 — The Miracle Prayer to Jesus

Lord Jesus, I come before You with a humble heart. Guide me in Your Spirit.

Prayer

Lord Jesus, I come before You, just as I am, I am sorry for my sins, I repent of my sins, please forgive me. In Your Name, I forgive all others for what they have done against me. I renounce Satan, the evil spirits and all their works. I give You my entire self, Lord Jesus, now and forever. I invite You into my life, Jesus. I accept You as my Lord, God and Savior. Heal me, change me, strengthen me in body, soul, and spirit.

Come Lord Jesus, cover me with Your Precious Blood, and fill me with Your Holy Spirit. I love You Lord Jesus. I praise You Jesus. I thank You Jesus. I shall follow You every day of my life. Amen.

The Miracle Prayer to Jesus

Day 19 — To St. Francis of Assisi

St. Francis, teach me simplicity, love, and peace.

Prayer

O St. Francis, gentle servant of God, help me live with humility and joy, protect the children and the poor, and guide my heart in courage, hope, and love.

Amen.

— *Saint Prayer (inspired)*

Day 20 — To Jesus, Lord of Mercy

Jesus, heal hearts and strengthen faith.

Prayer

O Jesus, Lord of Mercy,

heal the souls of the faithful departed,

protect my family, friends, and children,

and fill us with hope, courage, and love.

Amen.

— *Divine Mercy Devotion*

Day 21 — To St. Catherine of Siena

St. Catherine, inspire me with courage and wisdom.

Prayer

O St. Catherine of Siena,

teach me to speak and act with

courage and love,

help me trust in God's guidance,

and lead my heart to hope, patience,

and faith. Amen.

— *Prayer to St. Catherine of Siena*

Day 22 — To St. Ignatius of Loyola

St. Ignatius, help me discern God's will.

Prayer

O St. Ignatius, holy guide,

teach me to see God's plan in all things,

strengthen my heart with patience and courage,

and guide my steps in faith and obedience.

Amen.

— *Prayer to St. Ignatius of Loyola*

Day 23 — To St. Teresa of Calcutta (Mother Teresa)

St. Teresa, help me love selflessly.

Prayer

O St. Teresa of Calcutta, show me how to love and serve others, fill my heart with compassion and hope, and guide my actions in mercy and courage. Amen.

— *Prayer to St. Teresa of Calcutta*

Day 24 — To St. Joan of Arc

St. Joan, grant courage and faithfulness.

Prayer

O St. Joan of Arc, strengthen me to face challenges with courage, help me remain faithful to God's truth, and inspire hope and determination in my heart. Amen.

—*Prayer to St. Joan of Arc*

Day 25 — To Mary, Mother of the Church

Mother Mary, guide our families in faith and love.

Prayer

O Mary, Mother of the Church, protect my family, friends, and children, fill our hearts with love, hope, and patience, and lead us closer to Jesus in all we do. Amen.

— *Marian Devotion*

Day 26 — To St. Nicholas

St. Nicholas, protect children and bless families.

Prayer

God Our Father we pray,
That through the intercession of St. Nicholas,
You will protect our children.
Keep them safe from harm,

And help them grow,
And become worthy of Your sight.

Give them strength,
To keep their Faith in You,
And to keep alive their joy,
In Your creation.
Through Jesus Christ Our Lord.

Amen.

— *Prayer to St. Nicholas*

Day 27 — To St. Martin de Porres

St. Martin, teach me humility and kindness.

Prayer

O St. Martin de Porres, show me how to serve others with humility and love, help me grow in patience and courage, and lead me to trust God in all things. Amen.

— *Saint Prayer*

Day 28 — To St. Scholastica
St. Scholastica, guide me in prayer and devotion.

Prayer
O St. Scholastica, holy sister of God,
teach me to dedicate my life to prayer and love, fill my heart with hope and courage, and help me remain faithful to God's plan.
Amen.

— Saint Prayer to St. Scholastica

Day 29 — To St. Blaise
St. Blaise, protect us from sickness and harm.

Prayer
O St. Blaise, healer and protector,
watch over my health and the health of my loved ones,
grant courage, patience, and hope,

and guide us all in faith and trust in God.

Amen.

— *Prayer to St. Blaise*

Day 30 — To Jesus, Eternal Light

Jesus, fill our hearts with hope and courage.

Prayer

O Jesus, Eternal Light, shine upon the faithful departed, protect families, children, and friends, and fill our hearts with courage, love, and hope.
Amen.

— *Prayer for the departed and the families*

God's Wonderful Love

DECEMBER

Month of Advent

Month of the Nativity

Affirmation for the Month

In this month of Advent, I open my heart to hope, joy, and love. I prepare my soul to welcome Jesus, trusting in God's perfect timing and mercy.

DECEMBER

Day 1 — To Mary, Mother of Advent

Mary, gentle guide, teach me patience and hope.

Prayer

O Mary, Mother of Advent, prepare my heart to welcome Jesus, fill me with courage and trust, and help me walk faithfully in God's light.
Amen.

— *Marian Devotion*

Day 2 — To Jesus, Good Shepherd

Jesus, guide my heart and my steps.

Prayer

O Jesus, Good Shepherd, lead me in Your truth and love, protect my family, friends, and children, and fill me with hope, courage, and faith. Amen.

— *Advent Devotion*

Day 3 — To the Holy Spirit, Spirit of Joy

Holy Spirit, fill me with peace and guidance.

Prayer

Come, Holy Spirit, Spirit of Joy and Consolation, renew my heart with hope and trust, guide my thoughts and actions, and help me live with love, patience, and courage. Amen.

— *Holy Spirit Prayer*

Day 4 — In Honor of St. Nicholas

Loving God, help me follow the example of St. Nicholas in generosity and compassion.

Prayer

Loving God, we thank you for the example of St. Nicholas, who fed the hungry, brought hope to the imprisoned, gave comfort to the lost, and taught the truth to all. May we strive to imitate him by putting you first in all we do. Give us the courage, love and strength of St. Nicholas, so that, like him, we may serve you through loving our brothers and sisters. Amen.

— *Prayer in Honor of St. Nicholas*

Day 5 — To St. John Bosco
St. John Bosco, guide the young in faith and love.

Prayer
O St. John Bosco, protector of children and youth, help me guide the young with patience and wisdom, fill my heart with courage, hope, and joy, and lead all souls closer to God's love.
Amen.

— *Prayer to St John Bosco*

Day 6 — To Divine Mercy

Jesus, let Your mercy renew my heart and heal my wounds.

Prayer

O Divine Mercy of Jesus, pour Your loving kindness upon the world, heal the broken-hearted, protect the innocent, and fill our hearts with courage, hope, and faith. Amen.

— *Prayer for Mercy*

Day 7 — To St. Clare of Assisi

St. Clare, teach simplicity and devotion.

Prayer

O St. Clare, humble servant of God, help me walk with simplicity and love, strengthen my heart with patience and hope, and guide my actions in faith and devotion. Amen.

— *Prayer To St. Clare of Assisi*

Day 8 — To the Holy Spirit

Holy Spirit, fill me with wisdom and guidance.

Prayer

Come, Holy Spirit, illuminate my mind and guide my steps, grant me courage, patience, and understanding, and lead me closer to God's perfect will. Amen.

— *Prayer to the Holy Spirit*

Day 9 — To St. Lucy

St. Lucy, shine light upon my path.

Prayer

O St. Lucy, beacon of God's light, illuminate my thoughts and heart with hope, protect my family and loved ones, and fill my life with faith, courage, and joy. Amen.

— *Prayer to St. Lucy*

Day 10 — To St. Teresa of Avila

St. Teresa, inspire prayer and trust in God.

Prayer

O St. Teresa of Avila, teach me to pray with sincerity and devotion, strengthen my heart with hope and courage, and guide my soul in love and obedience to God.
Amen.

— *Prayer to St Teresa of Avila*

Day 11 — To Saint Joseph, Protector of Families

Saint Joseph, watch over my loved ones and home.

Prayer

Hail, Joseph, image of the Eternal Father;
Hail, Joseph, guardian of the Eternal Son;

Hail, Joseph, temple of the Eternal Spirit;
Hail, Joseph, beloved of the Trinity.
Hail, Joseph, spouse and companion of the Mother of God.
Hail, Joseph, friend of angels.
Hail, Joseph, believer in miracles.
Hail, Joseph, follower of dreams.
Hail, Joseph, lover of simplicity.
Hail, Joseph, exemplar of righteousness;
Hail, Joseph, model of meekness and patience;
Hail, Joseph, model of humility and obedience.
Blessed are the eyes that have seen what you saw.
Blessed are the ears that have heard what you heard.
Blessed are the arms that have embraced what you embraced.
Blessed is the lap that has held what

you held.
Blessed is the heart that has loved what you loved.
Blessed is the Father who chose you;
Blessed is the Son who loved you:
Blessed is the Spirit who sanctified you.
Blessed is Mary, your spouse, who honoured and loved you. Blessed is the angel who guarded and led you. And blessed be forever all who remember and honour you. O Saint Joseph, faithful guardian, guide our hearts in love,
keep us safe from harm, and teach us trust and patience in God. Amen.

— Hail Joseph

Day 12 — To Mary, Seat of Wisdom
Mary, guide my thoughts with clarity and peace.

Prayer

O Mary, Seat of Wisdom, enlighten my mind with understanding, help me choose what is good and pleasing to God, and fill my heart with patience, faith, and hope. Amen.

— *Maria Devotion*

Day 13 — To St. Gabriel the Archangel

St. Gabriel, messenger of God's hope, guide me to listen with faith and trust.

Prayer

O St. Gabriel, holy messenger, bring God's peace into my heart and home, strengthen me with courage and calm, and help me listen faithfully to God's voice.
Amen.

— *Prayer to St. Gabriel the Archangel*

Day 14 — To the Eucharistic Lord

Jesus present in the Eucharist, nourish my soul and strengthen my spirit.

Prayer

O Jesus in the Blessed Sacrament, fill my heart with Your healing presence, renew my strength in moments of weakness, and guide me in love, humility, and faith. Amen.

— *Prayer to the Eucharistic Lord*

Day 15 — To St. John the Apostle

St. John, teach me to love with a faithful heart.

Prayer

O St. John, beloved disciple, help me love others with truth and compassion, grant me a heart full of peace and courage, and guide me closer to the light of Christ. Amen.

DECEMBER

— *Prayer to St. John the Apostle*

Day 16 — To St. Benedict
St. Benedict, guard me against temptation.

Prayer
O St. Benedict, holy protector, shield me from harm and temptation, strengthen my spirit with discipline and peace, and guide me safely along God's holy path. Amen.

— *Prayer to St. Benedict*

Day 17 — To Divine Hope
Lord, fill my heart with unwavering hope.

Prayer
O Jesus, source of eternal hope, lift my heart when I am weary, fill me with courage to trust in Your timing, and

guide me in faith, patience, and love. Amen.

Divine Hope Prayer

Day 18 — To St. Anthony of Padua

St. Anthony, guide me to find God's wisdom.

Prayer

I salute you, St. Anthony, lily of purity, ornament and glory of Christianity.

I salute you, great Saint, cherub of wisdom and seraph of divine love. I rejoice at the favours Our Lord has so liberally bestowed on you.

In humility and confidence, I entreat you to help me, for I know that God has given you charity and compassion, as well as power.

I ask you, by the love you felt toward the Holy Infant Jesus as you held Him in your arms, to tell Him now of the favours I seek through your intercession. *(Mention your petition.)*

O glorious favourite of God, in humble reverence I petition you to grant me what I so urgently ask for, and I will make known your goodness and holiness, thereby to honour and glorify Him who has so greatly blessed you.
Amen.

O St. Anthony, gentle wonder-worker, bring peace to troubled hearts,
guide me in times of confusion and worry, and fill my life with clarity, trust, and hope.
Amen.

— *Prayer to St. Anthony in any necessity*

Day 19 — Daily Prayer to St. Nicholas
St. Nicholas, guide me in childlike faith, generosity, and joy

Prayer

O good St. Nicholas, you who are the joy of the children, put in my heart the spirit of childhood, which the gospel speaks, and teach me to seed happiness around me. You, whose feast prepares us for Christmas, open my faith to the mystery of God made man. You good bishop and shepherd, help me to find my place in the Church and inspire the Church to be faithful to the gospel.

O good Saint Nicholas, patron of children, sailors and the helpless, watch over those who pray to Jesus, your Lord and theirs, as well as over those who humble themselves before you. Bring us all in reverence to the Holy Child of Bethlehem, when true joy and peace are found. Amen.

— *Prayer to St. Nicholas*

Day 20 — Prayer to the Sacred Heart of Jesus

Jesus, shape my heart to be gentle, humble, and obedient to Your will.

Prayer

O most holy heart of Jesus, fountain of every blessing, I adore you, I love you, and with lively sorrow for my sins, I offer you this poor heart of mine. Make me humble, patient, pure and wholly obedient to your will. Grant, good Jesus, that I may live in you and for you. Protect me in the midst of danger. Comfort me in my afflictions. Give me health of body, assistance in my temporal needs, your blessing on all that I do, and the grace of a holy death. Amen

— *Prayer to Sacred Heart of Jesus*

Day 21 — To St. Raphael the Archangel

St. Raphael, bearer of healing and peace.

Prayer

O St. Raphael, gentle healer, bring God's peace into my heart and home, guide me toward strength, wholeness, and hope, and protect me on every path I walk. Amen.

— *Prayer to St. Raphael*

Day 22 — To the Holy Spirit, Giver of New Beginnings

Holy Spirit, renew my heart and my life.

Prayer

Come, Holy Spirit of Renewal, refresh my thoughts with clarity and peace, open doors to new opportunities and grace, and lead me forward with courage and joy. Amen.

DECEMBER

Day 23 — To St. Faustina

St. Faustina, witness of Divine Mercy, guide my heart in trust.

Prayer

O St. Faustina, teach me to trust in Jesus with a simple and humble heart, help me surrender my worries to His mercy, and fill my soul with hope, peace, and compassion for others. Amen

— Prayer to St. Faustina

Day 24 — To Jesus, Light of the Nations

Jesus, shine Your peace upon the world.

Prayer

O Jesus, Light of the Nations, fill the world with peace and healing, brighten my heart with hope and trust, and guide me to walk in Your love each day. Amen.

— Prayer to Jesus, Light of the Nations

Day 25 — To the Infant Jesus

O Infant Jesus, fill my heart with childlike faith and purity.

Prayer

O Jesus, Who has said, "Ask and you shall receive, seek and you shall find, knock and it shall be opened," through the intercession of Mary, Your Most Holy Mother, I knock, I seek, I ask that my prayer be granted.

(Make your request)

O Jesus, Who has said, "All that you ask of the Father in My Name, He will grant you," through the intercession of Mary Your Most Holy Mother, I humbly and urgently ask your Father in your name that my prayer will be granted.

(Make your request)

O Jesus, Who has said, "Heaven and earth shall pass away but My word shall not pass away," through the intercession of Mary Your Most Holy Mother, I feel confident that my prayer will be granted. (Make your request)

— *Infant Jesus of Prague Novena Prayer*

Day 26 — To Saint Joseph the Worker
Saint Joseph, humble worker and faithful protector. Bless my efforts today. My labour, my plans, and my decisions. Teach me to work with patience, dignity, and grace.

Prayer
O Saint Joseph, model of all who labour, sanctify my work and guide my hands. Help me offer every task, big or small, for the glory of God and the good of others. Amen.

— *Prayer to Saint Joseph the Worker (inspired)*

Day 27 — To Holy Spirit, giver of spiritual gifts and guidance.

Holy Spirit, fill my heart with Your presence, grace, and wisdom.

Prayer

Come, Holy Spirit, fill my heart with Your presence and grace. Grant me the gift of wisdom to see God's plan, the gift of understanding to know Your truth, the gift of counsel to make right choices, the gift of fortitude to face life with courage, the gift of knowledge to grow in faith, the gift of piety to love and serve You, and the gift of fear of the Lord to walk humbly in Your ways.

Holy Spirit, guide me in all I do, strengthen my heart, enlighten my mind, and help me live fully in God's love. Amen.

— *Prayer for the Gifts of the Holy Spirit.*

Day 28 — To the Holy Family

Jesus, Mary, and Joseph, bless and protect families.

Prayer

O Holy Family of Nazareth, watch over my home with love and peace, grant unity, patience, and courage to all families, and guide us to live in faith and kindness. Amen.

— Prayer to the Holy Family

Day 29 — To St. Bridget of Sweden

St. Bridget, model of prayerful strength, guide me to trust and persevere in all trials.

Prayer

O St. Bridget of Sweden, teach me to pray with sincerity and trust, help me remain strong in trials and hardship, and fill my heart with hope, courage, and peace. Amen.

— *Prayer to St. Bridget of Sweden*

Day 30 — To Heavenly Father, Divine Healer

Heavenly Father, Divine Healer, restore my soul and spirit.

Prayer

Loving Father, touch me now with your healing hands, for I believe that your will is for me to be well in mind, body, soul and spirit. Cover me with the most precious blood of your Son, our Lord, Jesus Christ from the top of my head to the soles of my feet.

— *From the Prayer attributed to St. Padre Pio*

Day 31 — To Jesus, My Strength and My Promise

Jesus, walk with me into every moment ahead.

DECEMBER

Prayer

O Jesus, my Strength and my Promise, fill my heart with courage for what is new, guide my steps with wisdom and peace, and help me begin the coming year with trust, love, and a faithful spirit. Amen.

Biblical Devotion

A Thanksgiving Prayer at Year's End

I end this year with gratitude and trust in God.

Prayer

O God, thank You for guiding me through this year. For the blessings that strengthened me, the challenges that shaped me, and the mercy that carried me.

Stay with me as I step into a new year. Fill my heart with peace, hope, and courage, and help me walk faithfully in Your love.

Amen.

Daily Affirmation — Health, Wealth, Love, and Success

I am blessed by God in body, mind, and spirit.
He fills my body with strength and vitality.
His wisdom guides my choices in work and life.
His love surrounds my heart, family, and friends.
I walk in faith, courage, and hope,
and God leads me toward success, peace, and joy.

Prayer for Courage

Jesus, strengthen my heart with Your courage.
When I feel afraid or uncertain,
remind me that You walk beside me.

Fill my mind with peace,
my soul with confidence,
and my steps with boldness.

Help me face each challenge
with faith, trust, and hope in You.
Amen.

Prayer for the Gifts of the Holy Spirit

Come, Holy Spirit,
fill my heart with Your presence and grace.

Grant me the gift of **wisdom** to see God's plan,
the gift of **understanding** to know Your truth,
the gift of **counsel** to make right choices,
the gift of **fortitude** to face life with courage,
the gift of **knowledge** to grow in faith,
the gift of **piety** to love and serve You,

and the gift of **fear of the Lord** to walk humbly in Your ways.

Holy Spirit, guide me in all I do,
strengthen my heart, enlighten my mind,
and help me live fully in God's love.
Amen.

Prayer for the Fruits of the Holy Spirit

Come, Holy Spirit,
fill my heart with Your presence and love.

Grant me the fruits of Your Spirit:
love to care for others sincerely,
joy to rejoice in Your blessings,
peace to calm my heart in every moment,
patience to endure trials with grace,
kindness to serve others with compassion,
goodness to choose what is holy and

true, **faithfulness** to remain steadfast in Your ways, **gentleness** to act with humility, and **self-control** to follow God's will.

Holy Spirit, guide me each day,
that my life may reflect Your love and goodness.
Amen.

Prayer Before Work

My Heavenly Father, as I enter this workplace, I bring your presence with me.

I speak your peace, your grace, your mercy and your perfect order into my work.
I acknowledge your power over all that will be done, spoken, thought and decided within these walls.

Lord, I thank you for the gifts you have blessed me with.
I commit to use them responsibly in your honour.

Give me a fresh supply of strength to do my job.
Anoint my projects, ideas, and energy, so that even my smallest accomplishment may bring you glory.

Lord, when I am confused, guide me.
When I am weary, energize me.
When I am burned out, infuse me with the light of the Holy Spirit.

May the work that I do and the way I do it bring faith, joy and a smile to all that I come in contact with today.

And oh Lord, When I leave this place, give me traveling mercy.
Bless my family and home to be in order as I left it.

Lord, I thank you for everything you've done, everything you are doing, and everything you are going to do.

In the name of Jesus I pray, with much love and thanksgiving.
In the name of the Father, and of the Son, and of the Holy Spirit, Amen

Infant Jesus of Prague Novena Prayer

O Jesus, Who has said, "Ask and you shall receive, seek and you shall find, knock and it shall be opened," through the intercession of Mary, Your Most Holy Mother, I knock, I seek, I ask that my prayer be granted.
(Make your request)
O Jesus, Who has said, "All that you ask of the Father in My Name, He will grant you," through the intercession of Mary Your Most Holy Mother, I humbly and urgently ask your Father in your name

that my prayer will be granted.
(Make your request)
O Jesus, Who has said, "Heaven and earth shall pass away but My word shall not pass away," through the intercession of Mary Your Most Holy Mother, I feel confident that my prayer will be granted.
(Make your request)

Prayer to the Holy Family

Dear Lord,
Bless our family.
Be so kind as to give us the unity, peace, and mutual love that You found in Your own family in the little town of Nazareth.

Saint Joseph,
pray for the head of our family.
Obtain for him the strength, the wisdom, and the prudence he needs

to support and direct those under his care.

Mother Mary,
pray for the mother of our family.
Help her to be pure and kind,
gentle and self-sacrificing.
For the more she resembles you,
the better will our family be.

Lord Jesus,
bless the children of our family.
Help them to be obedient and
devoted to their parents.
Make them more and more like You.
Let them grow, as You did,
in wisdom and strength and grace
before God and man.

Holy Family of Nazareth,
by your intercession, love, and holy
example, make our family and home
more and more like Yours,

until we are all one family,
happy and at peace
in our true home with You. Amen.

Chaplet of Divine Mercy

Opening Prayers:

Begin with the Sign of the Cross.
Then pray: **Divine Mercy 3 O' Clock** Prayer

"You expired, Jesus, but the source of life gushed forth for souls, and the ocean of mercy opened up for the whole world. O Fount of Life, unfathomable Divine Mercy, envelop the whole world and empty Yourself out upon us."

Optional Opening Prayers:

- Our Father
- Hail Mary
- The Apostles' Creed

On the Large Beads (Our Father Beads):

"Eternal Father, I offer You the Body and Blood, Soul and Divinity of Your dearly beloved Son, Our Lord Jesus Christ, in atonement for our sins and those of the whole world."

On the Small Beads (Hail Mary Beads):

"For the sake of His sorrowful Passion, have mercy on us and on the whole world."

Closing Prayer:

"Holy God, Holy Mighty One, Holy Immortal One, have mercy on us and on the whole world." (Repeat three times)

Optional Final Prayer:

"Eternal God, in whom mercy is endless and the treasury of compassion — inexhaustible, look kindly upon us and increase Your mercy in us, that in difficult moments we might not despair nor become despondent, but with

great confidence submit ourselves to Your holy will, which is Love and Mercy itself. Amen."

The Apostles' Creed

I believe in God, the Father Almighty,
Creator of heaven and earth.

And in Jesus Christ, His only Son, our Lord,
who was conceived by the Holy Spirit,
born of the Virgin Mary,
suffered under Pontius Pilate,
was crucified, died, and was buried;
He descended into hell;
on the third day He rose again from the dead;
He ascended into heaven,
and is seated at the right hand of God the Father Almighty;
from there He will come to judge the living and the dead.

I believe in the Holy Spirit,
the holy Catholic Church,
the communion of saints,
the forgiveness of sins,
the resurrection of the body,
and life everlasting.
Amen.

The Lord's Prayer

Our Father, Who art in
heaven, Hallowed be Thy Name.
Thy Kingdom come.
Thy Will be done,
on earth as it is in Heaven.

Give us this day our daily bread.
And forgive us our trespasses,
as we forgive those who trespass
against us. Lead us not into
temptation, but deliver us from evil.
Amen.

Rosary:
How to Pray the Rosary

1. Make the Sign of the Cross.
2. On the crucifix, pray the Apostles' Creed.
3. On the first large bead, pray the Our Father.
4. On the next three small beads, pray Hail Mary for Faith, Hope, and Charity.
5. Say the Glory Be.
6. Announce the first mystery.
7. On the large bead, pray the Our Father.
8. On the ten small beads, pray Hail Marys while meditating on the mystery.
9. After each decade, pray:

"O My Jesus, forgive us our sins, save us from the fires of hell, and lead all souls to Heaven, especially those in most need of Your mercy."

10. Repeat for all five decades.

11. Conclude with the Hail Holy Queen and any additional prayers.

Joyful Mysteries — Monday & Saturday

1. The Annunciation of the Angel to Mary.

The angel Gabriel was sent from God to a town of Galilee called Nazareth. And coming to Mary, he said, "Hail Mary full of grace, the Lord is with you."

Reflection: Trust God's plan for my life.

2. The Visitation of Mary to Saint Elizabeth.

Mary set out and travelled to the house of Zechariah and greeted Elizabeth. When Elizabeth heard Mary's greeting, the infant leaped in her womb, and Elizabeth, filled with the Holy Spirit,

cried out in a loud voice and said,
"Most blessed are you among women,
and blessed is the fruit of your womb."

Reflection: Serve others with love and compassion.

3. The Nativity of Jesus in Bethlehem

And Mary gave birth to her firstborn son. She wrapped him in swaddling clothes and laid him in a manger . And suddenly there was a multitude of the heavenly host praising God and saying: "Glory to God in the highest and on earth peace to those on whom his favour rests."

Reflection: God's love comes humbly into the world.

4. The Presentation of Jesus to the Temple.

Mary and Joseph took the baby Jesus to the Temple to present him to the Lord. At the temple Simeon and Anna came forward, gave thanks to God and spoke about Jesus to all who were present.

Reflection: Offer my life to God in gratitude and faith.

5. The Finding of Jesus in the Temple

The boy Jesus remained behind in Jerusalem, but his parents did not know it. After three days they found him in the temple, sitting in the midst of the teachers, listening to them and asking them questions.

Reflection: Seek God's wisdom and share it with others.

Sorrowful Mysteries — Tuesday & Friday

1. The Agony in the Garden

Jesus went to a place called Gethsemane to pray. "My Father, if it is possible, let this cup pass from me; yet, not as I will, but as you will."

Reflection: Trust God in trials.

2. The Scourging at the Pillar

The chief priests with the elders and the scribes held a council. They bound Jesus, led him away, and handed him over to Pilate. Pilate, wishing to satisfy the crowd, had Jesus scourged and handed him over to be crucified.

Reflection: Endure suffering with patience.

3. The Crowning with Thorns

They stripped off his clothes and threw a scarlet military cloak about him. Weaving a crown out of thorns, they placed it on his head, and a reed in his right hand. And kneeling before him, they mocked him, saying, "Hail, King of the Jews!"

Reflection: Embrace humility and love.

4. The Carrying of the Cross

Jesus, weak from being beaten, was unable to carry His cross to Golgotha alone. Simon, a Cyrenian, helped him.

Reflection: Persevere in faith through difficulties.

5. The Crucifixion

When they came to the place called The Skull, they crucified him there, along with the criminals one on his right, the other on his left. And Jesus said, "Father, forgive them, for they know not what they do."...It was now about the sixth hour, and there was darkness over the whole land until the ninth hour, while the sun's light failed; and the curtain of the temple was torn into two. Then Jesus, crying with a loud voice, said "Father, into thy hands I commit my spirit!" and having said this he breathed His last.

Reflection: Unite my sufferings with Christ's love.

Glorious Mysteries — Wednesday & Sunday

1. The Resurrection of our Lord.

Mary Magdalene and the other Mary came to see the tomb. An angel appeared and said, "Do not be afraid! I know that you are seeking Jesus the crucified. He is not here, for He has been raised just as He said."

Reflection: Christ brings hope and eternal life.

2. The Ascension of our Lord.

As Jesus blessed them He parted from them and was taken up to heaven.

Reflection: Keep my heart set on God's Kingdom.

3. The Descent of the Holy Spirit

Holy Spirit came upon Mother Mary and the Apostles in Jerusalem, empowering them with courage, understanding, and the ability to speak in other tongues (languages).

'And when the day of Pentecost was fully come, they were all with one accord in one place. And suddenly there came a sound from heaven as of a rushing mighty wind, and it filled all the house where they were sitting. And there appeared unto them cloven tongues like as of fire, and it sat upon each of them. And they were all filled with the Holy

Ghost, and began to speak with other tongues, as the Spirit gave them utterance.'

Reflection: Open my heart to the Spirit's gifts.

4. The Assumption of the Blessed Virgin Mary into Heaven.

"Finally, the Immaculate Virgin, preserved free from all stain of original sin, when the course of her earthly life was finished, was taken up body and soul into heavenly glory."

Reflection: Honor Mary's faithful life.

5. The Coronation of the Blessed Virgin Mary, Queen of Heaven and Earth

"We believe that the Holy Mother of God, Mother of the Church, continues in heaven to exercise her maternal role on behalf of the members of Christ."

Reflection: Strive for holiness and union with God.

Luminous Mysteries — Thursday

1. The Baptism of Jesus

And a voice came from the heavens, saying, "This is my beloved Son, with whom I am well pleased."

Reflection: Live a life of holiness and renewal.

2. The Wedding at Cana

"Women, how does your concern affect me? My hour has not yet come." His mother said to the servers, "Do whatever he tells you."

Reflection: Trust in God's timing and Mary's intercession.

3. Proclamation of the Kingdom

"This is the time of fulfillment. The kingdom of God is at hand. Repent, and believe in the gospel."

Reflection: Share the Good News with joy.

4. The Transfiguration

While he was praying his face changed in appearance and his clothing became dazzling white.

Reflection: Be transformed by God's love.

5. The Institution of the Eucharist

Before the feast of Passover, Jesus knew that his hour had come to pass from this world to the Father. He loved his own in the world, and he loved them to the end.

Reflection: Receive Christ in the Eucharist with love.

Hail Holy Queen

Hail, Holy Queen, Mother of Mercy,

Hail our life, our sweetness, and our hope.

To you do we cry, poor banished children of Eve.

To you do we send up our sighs,

mourning and weeping in this valley of tears.

Turn then, most gracious Advocate,

your eyes of mercy toward us,

and after this our exile,

show unto us the blessed fruit of thy womb, Jesus.

O clement, O loving, O sweet Virgin Mary.

"Pray for us, O Holy Mother of God, that we may be made worthy of the promises of Christ."

Let Us Pray

O God, whose only-begotten Son, by His life, death, and resurrection, has purchased for us the rewards of eternal life, grant, we beseech You, that meditating upon these mysteries of the Most Holy Rosary of the Blessed Virgin Mary, we may imitate what they contain and obtain what they promise, through the same Christ our Lord. Amen.

Litany of the Blessed Virgin Mary (Litany of Loreto)

Lord, have mercy on us.
Lord, have mercy on us.
Christ, have mercy on us.
Christ, have mercy on us.
Lord, have mercy on us.
Lord, have mercy on us.
Christ, hear us.
Christ, graciously hear us.

God the Father of Heaven, **have mercy on us.**
God the Son, Redeemer of the world, **have mercy on us.**
God the Holy Spirit, **have mercy on us.**
Holy Trinity, One God, **have mercy on us.**

Invocation of Mary

(Pray for us)

Holy Mary, **pray for us.**
Holy Mother of God
Holy Virgin of virgins

Mother of Christ
Mother of the Church
Mother of Divine Grace
Mother most pure
Mother most chaste
Mother inviolate
Mother undefiled
Mother most amiable
Mother most admirable
Mother of good counsel
Mother of our Creator
Mother of our Saviour

Virgin most prudent
Virgin most venerable
Virgin most renowned
Virgin most powerful

Virgin most merciful
Virgin most faithful

Mirror of justice
Seat of wisdom
Cause of our joy
Spiritual vessel
Vessel of honor
Singular vessel of devotion
Mystical Rose
Tower of David
Tower of ivory
House of gold
Ark of the Covenant
Gate of Heaven
Morning Star

Health of the sick
Refuge of sinners
Comforter of the afflicted
Help of Christians

Queen of Angels

Queen of Patriarchs

Queen of Prophets

Queen of Apostles

Queen of Martyrs

Queen of Confessors

Queen of Virgins

Queen of all Saints

Queen conceived without original sin

Queen assumed into heaven

Queen of the most holy Rosary

Queen of families

Queen of peace

Lamb of God, who takes away the sins of the world, **spare us, O Lord.**
Lamb of God, who takes away the sins of the world, **graciously hear us, O Lord.**
Lamb of God, who takes away the sins of the world, **have mercy on us.**

We Fly to Your Patronage

We fly to your patronage, O holy Mother of God; do not despise our petitions in our necessities, but deliver us always from all dangers, O glorious and blessed Virgin.
Amen.

Saints
(pray for us)

St. Peter, **pray for us.**
St. Paul
St. Andrew
St. James
St. John
St. Thomas
St. James the Less
St. Philip
St. Bartholomew
St. Matthew

St. Simon

St. Thaddeus (St. Jude)

All you holy apostles and evangelists

All you holy disciples of our Lord

All you holy innocents

St. Stephen

St. Lawrence

St. Vincent

St. Fabian and St. Sebastian

St. John and St. Paul

St. Cosmas and St. Damian

All you holy martyrs

St. Sylvester

St. Gregory

St. Ambrose

St. Augustine

St. Jerome

All you holy bishops and confessors

God's Wonderful Love

St. Anthony
St. Benedict
St. Bernard
St. Dominic
St. Francis

Find Prayer:

Prayer of Gratitude for Daily Blessings 7

Prayer of Gratitude for Life's Abundance 8

Prayer of Gratitude for Guidance and Relationships 10

Prayer of Gratitude for Strength, Courage, and Purpose 12

Prayer of Gratitude for Family, Peace, and Blessings 14

Prayer of Gratitude for Health, Vitality, and Joy 16

Prayer of Gratitude for Life's Journey 18

New Year Blessing 20

JANUARY 21

   Day 1 — To God Our Father 22

   Day 2 — To the Blessed Virgin Mary, Mother of God 22

   Day 3 — To the Holy Spirit, Comforter and Guide 23

   Day 4 — To My Guardian Angel, Heavenly Protector 24

   Day 5 — To the Holy Family 25

   Day 6 — Feast of the Epiphany 25

   Day 7 — To Divine Mercy 26

Day 8 — To the Sacred Heart of Jesus .. 26

Day 9 — To Saint Joseph, Protector of Families 27

Day 10 — To the Blessed Virgin Mary, Comforter 28

Day 11 — To Saint Agnes, Pure and Faithful 28

Day 12 — To the Guardian Angel 29

Day 13 — To Mother Mary, Star of the Sea 30

Day 14 — To Jesus, Light of the World .. 30

Day 15 — To the Holy Spirit, Source of Wisdom 31

Day 16 — To Saint Blaise, Protector of Health 31

Day 17 — To Saint Francis de Sales, Patron of Gentle Hearts 32

Day 18 — To Mother Mary, Comforter of Souls 33

Day 19 — To Jesus, Divine Physician 34

Day 20 — To the Holy Spirit, Consoler of Hearts 34

Day 21 — To Saint Joseph, Terror of Demons 35

Day 22 — To Mother Mary, Queen of Angels 36

Day 23 — To Jesus, Bread of Life 36

Day 24 — To Saint Valentine, Intercessor for Love 37

Day 25 — Prayer for Serenity and Peace 38

Day 26 — To Mother Mary, Help of Christians 38

Day 27 — To the Holy Spirit, Advocate and Guide 39

Day 28 — To Jesus, Prince of Peace 40

Day 29 — To Saint George, Defender of Faith 40

Day 30 — To the Sacred Heart of Jesus 41

Day 31 — To Divine Mercy 42

FEBRUARY 43

Day 1 — To the Holy Family 44

Day 2 — To the Blessed Virgin Mary, Our Lady of Lourdes 44

Day 3 — To the Holy Spirit, Giver of Courage 45

Day 4 — To Saint Blaise, Protector of Health 46

Day 5 — To the Sacred Heart of Jesus .. 46

Day 6 — To Saint Joseph, Protector of Families 47

Day 7 — To the Holy Spirit, Fire of Love 48

Day 8 — To the Immaculate Heart of Mary 48

Day 9 — To the Divine Mercy of Jesus .. 49

Day 10 — To Saint George, Defender of Faith 50

Day 11 — To Mother Mary, Destroyer of the Devil 50

Day 12 — To Jesus, Healer of the Brokenhearted 51

Day 13 — To Saint Michael the Archangel 52

Day 14 — To the Sacred Heart of Jesus (Feast of Love) 53

Day 15 — Prayer for Serenity 53

Day 16 — To the Holy Spirit, Spirit of Truth 54

Day 17 — To Saint Bernadette of Lourdes 55

Day 18 — To the Holy Cross 55

Day 19 — To Jesus, the Good Shepherd 56

Day 20 — To Saint Peter, Keeper of Faith 57

Day 21 — To Mother Mary, Our Lady of Fatima 57

Day 22 — To the Holy Spirit, Breath of Life 58

Day 23 — To the Eucharistic Heart of Jesus 59

Day 24 — To the Guardian Angel 59

Day 25 — To Saint Therese of Lisieux ... 60

Day 26 — To the Precious Blood of Jesus 60

Day 27 — To Saint Gabriel the Archangel 61

Day 28 — To Jesus, King of Mercy 62

Day 29 — To the Holy Family (Leap Year Blessing) 62

MARCH 64

  Day 1 — To Saint Joseph, Guardian of the Redeemer 65

  Day 2 — To Jesus, the Light of the World 65

  Day 3 — To the Holy Spirit, Spirit of Wisdom 66

  Day 5 — To Saint Joseph the Worker 68

  Day 7 — To the Holy Spirit, Giver of Courage 69

  Day 8 — To Mother Mary, Our Lady of Fatima 70

  Day 9 — To Jesus, Fountain of Mercy ... 71

  Day 10 — To the Guardian Angel 71

  Day 11 — To Saint Joseph, Pillar of Families 72

  Day 12 — To Saint Michael the Archangel 73

  Day 13 — To Jesus, My Peace 74

  Day 14 — The Fatima Prayer 74

  Day 15 — To God, the Source of Serenity 75

Day 16 — To Saint Joseph, Protector of the Church 76

Day 17 — To Saint Patrick, Apostle of Ireland 76

Day 18 — To Mother Mary, Star of the Sea 78

Day 19 — Solemnity of Saint Joseph, Spouse of the Blessed Virgin Mary 78

Day 20 — To Jesus, the Bread of Life 79

Day 21 — To the Holy Spirit, Giver of Hope 80

Day 22 — To Saint Gabriel the Archangel 80

Day 23 — To Saint Joseph, Model of Patience 81

Day 24 — To the Blessed Trinity 81

Day 25 — The Annunciation to Mother Mary 82

Day 26 — To Saint Joseph, Mirror of Charity.. 83

Day 27 — To Saint George, Courageous Martyr.. 84

Day 28 — To Jesus, the Sacred Heart ... 84

Day 29 — To the Holy Spirit, Spirit of Renewal... 85

Day 30 — To Saint Joseph, Terror of Demons... 86

Day 31 — To Jesus, My Redeemer 86

APRIL..88

Day 1 — To Jesus in the Holy Eucharist 89

Day 2 — To the Risen Christ 89

Day 3 — To the Holy Spirit, Bringer of Renewal... 90

Day 4 — To the Sacred Heart of Jesus .. 90

Day 5 — To Mary, Mother of the Risen Lord... 91

Day 6 — Holy Spirit Prayer of Saint Augustine.. 92

Day 7 — To Jesus, the Good Shepherd . 93

Day 8 — To the Holy Spirit, Spirit of Truth 93

Day 9 — To the Divine Mercy of Jesus .. 94

Day 10 — To Saint Joseph, Protector of Families.. 95

Day 11 — To the Precious Blood of Jesus 95

Day 12 — To the Guardian Angel 96
Day 13 — To Mary, Queen of Peace 96
Day 14 — To Jesus, the Healer 97
Day 15 — To the Holy Spirit, Giver of Courage 98
Day 16 — To the Cross of Christ 98
Day 17 — To Saint Patrick, Apostle of Ireland 99
Day 18 — To the Immaculate Heart of Mary 100
Day 19 — To Saint George, Defender of Faith 101
Day 20 — To Jesus, Prince of Peace ... 101
Day 21 — To the Holy Spirit, Fire of Love 102
Day 22 — To Mary, Mother of Hope 103
Day 23 — To Mary, Undoer of Knots ... 103
Day 24 — To the Saints 104
Day 25 — To Jesus, the King of Glory.. 104
Day 26 — To the Holy Spirit, Comforter 105
Day 27 — To Saint Joseph the Worker 105

Day 28 — To the Holy Eucharist (Act of Love) 106

Day 29 — To Mary Magdalene, Witness of the Resurrection 107

Day 30 — To the Most Holy Trinity, Source of All Grace 107

MAY 109

Day 1 — To Mary, Mother of God 110

Day 2 — To Mary, Queen of Heaven ... 110

Day 3 — To the Holy Spirit, Spirit of Guidance 111

Day 4 — To Mother Mary, Our Lady of Fatima 112

Day 5 — To Jesus, Divine Mercy 112

Day 6 — To Saint Joseph, Guardian of the Redeemer 113

Day 7 — To the Guardian Angel 113

Day 8 — To Mary, Mother of Sorrows.. 114

Day 9 — To Saint Michael the Archangel 114

Day 10 — To Jesus, the Good Shepherd 115

Day 11 — To the Holy Spirit, Spirit of Wisdom 116

Day 12 — To Mary, Queen of Peace ... 116

Day 13 — To Saint Joseph, Model of Workers 117

Day 14 — To Jesus, the Lamb of God . 117

Day 15 — To Mary, Undoer of Knots ... 118

Day 16 — To Saint George, Defender of Faith 119

Day 17 — To Jesus, Sacred Heart 119

Day 18 — To the Holy Spirit, Comforter 120

Day 19 — To the Guardian Angel 120

Day 20 — To Mary, Mother of Mercy ... 121

Day 21 — To Jesus, Light of the World 121

Day 22 — To Saint Joseph, Pillar of Families 122

Day 23 — To the Holy Spirit, Spirit of Hope 123

Day 24 — To Mary, Star of the Sea 123

Day 25 — To Jesus, Risen Lord 124

Day 26 — To Saint Michael the Archangel 124

Day 27 — To Jesus, Divine Healer 125

Day 28 — To the Holy Spirit, Fire of Love 125

Day 29 — To Mary, Our Lady of Grace 126

Day 30 — To Jesus, Bread of Life 126

Day 31 — To the Blessed Trinity 127

JUNE 128

Day 1 — To the Sacred Heart of Jesus 129

Day 2 — To Jesus in the Holy Eucharist 129

Day 3 — To the Holy Spirit, Spirit of Love 130

Day 4 — To Heavenly Father, Divine Healer 131

Day 5 — To the Holy Spirit, Giver of Strength 131

Day 6 — To Mary, Mother of Mercy 133

Day 7 — To the Guardian Angel 134

Day 8 — To Saint Joseph, Protector of Families 134

Day 9 — To Jesus, Prince of Peace 135

Day 10 — To the Holy Spirit, Comforter 136

Day 11 — To Mary, Queen of Heaven . 136

Day 12 — To Jesus, Light of the World 137

Day 13 — To Saint Michael the Archangel 138

Day 14 — To Mary, Undoer of Knots ... 138

Day 15 — To Jesus, the Good Shepherd 139

Day 16 — To the Holy Spirit, Spirit of Wisdom 139

Day 17 — To Jesus, Divine Mercy 141

Day 18 — To Saint George, Defender of Faith 141

Day 19 — To Mary, Mother of the Church 142

Day 20 — To Jesus, Healer of the Sick 143

Day 21 — To the Holy Spirit, Spirit of Courage 143

Day 22 — To Mary, Star of the Sea 144

Day 23 — To Jesus, Prince of Peace ... 144

Day 24 — To Saint Joseph, Pillar of Families 145

Day 25 — To the Guardian Angel 145

Day 26 — To Christ, My Refuge and Strength 146

Day 27 — To the Lord, My Protector ... 147

Day 28 — To the Holy Spirit, Fire of Love 148

Day 29 — To Mary, Undoer of Knots ... 149

Day 30 — To Jesus, My Lord and All 149

JULY 151

Day 1 — To Jesus, Redeemer of Souls 152

Day 2 — To the Holy Spirit, Spirit of Courage 152

Day 3 — To Mary, Mother of Sorrows .. 153

Day 4 — To Jesus, the Perfume of Love and Sacrifice 153

Day 5 — To Mary, Queen of Heaven ... 154

Day 6 — To the Holy Spirit, Spirit of Wisdom 155

Day 7 — To Saint Joseph, Protector of Families 155

Day 8 — To God, Source of Wisdom and Peace 158

Day 9 — To the Guardian Angel 159

Day 10 — To Saint Patrick, Apostle of Ireland 160

Day 11 — To Jesus, the Good Shepherd 161

Day 12 — To the Holy Spirit, Spirit of Strength... 162

Day 13 — To Jesus, Divine Mercy 162

Day 14 — To Saint Michael the Archangel 163

Day 15 — To Mary, Mother of Hope 163

Day 16 — To Jesus, Bread of Life 164

Day 17 — To the Holy Spirit, Spirit of Guidance 164

Day 18 — To Saint Joseph, Worker and Protector... 165

Day 19 — To Jesus, Light of the World 166

Day 20 — To Mary, Queen of Peace ... 166

Day 21 — To Jesus, Healer of the Sick 167

Day 22 — To the Holy Spirit, Spirit of Love 168

Day 23 — To Mary, Mother of Consolation 168

Day 24 — To Jesus, the Good Shepherd 169

Day 25 — Prayer to St. Thomas Aquinas 169

Day 26 — Prayer to the Sacred Heart of Jesus 170

Day 27 — To Jesus, Divine Mercy 171

Day 28 — To the Holy Spirit, Comforter of Souls 171

Day 29 — To Saint Joseph, Guardian of the Redeemer 172

Day 30 — To the God of Infinite Mercy 172

Day 31 — To Jesus, the Redeemer 173

AUGUST 174

Day 1 — To Mary, Immaculate Heart .. 175

Day 2 — To St. Jude, Helper in Times of Need 175

Day 3 — To the Holy Spirit, Spirit of Peace 176

Day 4 — To Mary, Queen of Angels 177

Day 5 — To Jesus, Victor over Evil 177

Day 6 — To the Holy Spirit, Spirit of Guidance 178

Day 7 — To Saint Joseph, Model of Obedience 179

Day 8 — To Mary, Mother of Hope 179

Day 9 — To Saint Blaise, Protector of Health 180

Day 10 — To the Guardian Angel 180

Day 11 — To Jesus, Healer of the Brokenhearted 181

Day 12 — To the Precious Blood of Jesus 182

Day 13 — To the Holy Spirit, Spirit of Courage 182

Day 14 — To Saint Michael the Archangel 183

Day 15 — To Mary, Mother of Consolation 183

Day 16 — To Saint Francis de Sales, Patron of Gentle Hearts 184

Day 17 — To the Holy Spirit, Spirit of Wisdom 185

Day 18 — To Christ, My Refuge and Strength 185

Day 19 — To God Our Father 186

Day 20 — To the Blessed Virgin Mary, Mother of God 187

Day 21 — To the Guardian Angel 188

Day 22 — To Saint Agnes, Pure and Faithful 189

Day 23 — To Jesus, Victor over Evil 190

Day 24 — To the Holy Spirit, Spirit of Hope 190

Day 25 — To the Holy Spirit, Consoler of Hearts 191

Day 26 — To Saint Joseph, Terror of Demons 192

Day 27 — To Mother Mary, Queen of Angels 192

Day 28 — To the Holy Spirit, Spirit of Courage 193

Day 29 — To Mary, Mother of Perpetual Help 194

Day 30 — To the Blessed Virgin Mary, Our Lady of Lourdes 194

Day 31 — To Saint George, Defender of Faith 195

SEPTEMBER 196

Day 1 — To Mary, Mother of Sorrows .. 197

Day 2 — To Jesus, Comforter in Suffering 197

Day 3 — Prayer to the Sacred Heart of Jesus 198

Day 4 — To St. Joseph, Strong Protector 199

Day 5 — To Mary, Mother of Consolation 200

Day 6 — To Jesus, Divine Healer 201

Day 7 — To the Holy Spirit, Spirit of Guidance 201

Day 8 — Celebrating the Nativity Feast of Mary 202

Day 9 — To Our Father in Heaven 202

Day 10 — To Saint Patrick, Apostle of Ireland 203

Day 11 — To God, My Eternal Father .. 204

Day 12 — To the Holy Spirit, Spirit of Hope 205

Day 13 — To Jesus, the Good Shepherd 206

Day 14 — To God, My Companion in Every Moment 207

Day 15 — To St. Jude, Bearer of Hope in Hard Times 208

Day 16 — To Saint Gabriel the Archangel 209

Day 17 — To Saint George, Courageous Martyr 209

Day 18 — To Mother Mary, Destroyer of the Devil 210

Day 19 — To Jesus, Healer of the Heart 211

Day 20 — To the Holy Spirit, Giver of Every Good Fruit 211

Day 21 — To Mary, Mother of Consolation 212

Day 22 — To Jesus, Bread of Life 213

Day 23 — To St. John Bosco 213

Day 24 — To Divine Mercy.................. 214

Day 25 — To St. Clare of Assisi.......... 215

Day 26 — To the Holy Spirit, giver of light and life.. 215

Day 27 — To St. Lucy 216

Day 28 — To Mary, Undoer of Knots ... 216

Day 28 — To Mary, Mother of All Children 217

Day 29 — To the Infant Jesus............. 217

Day 30 — To St. Stephen the Martyr... 218

OCTOBER 219

Day 1 — To Mary, Seat of Wisdom 220

Day 2 — To the Eucharistic Lord........ 220

Day 3 — To St. John the Apostle 221

Day 4 — Prayer To St. Benedict 222

Day 5 — To Divine Hope 222

Day 6— To St. Anthony of Padua 223

Day 7 — To the Holy Spirit, Spirit of Strength.. 223

Day 8 — To St. Andrew the Apostle.... 224

Day 9 — To St. Raphael the Archangel 224

Day 10— To the Holy Spirit, Giver of New Beginnings 225

Day 11 — To St. Faustina 225

Day 12 — To Jesus, Light of the Nations 226

Day 13— To the Infant Jesus 227

Day 14 — To St. Stephen the Martyr ... 227

Day 15 — To St. John the Baptist 228

Day 16 — To the Holy Family 228

Day 17 — To St. Bridget of Sweden 229

Day 18 — To the Holy Spirit, Spirit of Protection 229

Day 19 — To Mary, Help of Christians 230

Day 20 — To the Holy Spirit, Spirit of Joy 230

Day 21 — To Mary, Mother of All Children 231

Day 22 — To Jesus, King of Glory 231

Day 26 — To Mary, Queen of the Holy Rosary 232

Day 27 — To Jesus, Shepherd of Souls 232

Day 28 — Anima Christi 233

Day 29 — To Saint Patrick, Apostle of Ireland 234

Day 30— To St. Francis of Assisi 235

Day 31 — To St. John the Baptist 236

NOVEMBER 237

Day 1 — To our Father, prayer for eternal rest... 238

Day 2 — To Mary, Mother of the Faithful 238

Day 3 — To the Holy Spirit, Spirit of Healing 239

Day 4 — To Saint Michael the Archangel 240

Day 5 — To Mary, Queen of Souls 240

Day 6 — To Heavenly Father, Divine Healer 241

Day 7 — To the Guardian Angel 242

Day 8 — To Mary, Mother of Hope...... 242

Day 9 — To Jesus, Divine Protector.... 243

Day 10 — To the Holy Spirit, Spirit of Hope 243

Day 11 — To Saint Joseph, Protector of Families... 244

Day 12 — To St. Jude, Patron of Hope 245

Day 13 — To Mary, Mother of Mercy ... 245

Day 14 — To St. Anthony of Padua 246

Day 15 — To Jesus, Divine Protector .. 247

Day 16 — To the Holy Spirit, Spirit of Guidance 248

Day 17 — To St. Therese of Lisieux 249

Day 18 — The Miracle Prayer to Jesus 249

Day 19 — To St. Francis of Assisi 250

Day 20 — To Jesus, Lord of Mercy 251

Day 22 — To St. Ignatius of Loyola 252

Day 23 — To St. Teresa of Calcutta (Mother Teresa) 252

Day 24 — To St. Joan of Arc 253

Day 25 — To Mary, Mother of the Church 254

Day 26 — To St. Nicholas 254

Day 27 — To St. Martin de Porres 255

Day 28 — To St. Scholastica 256

Day 29 — To St. Blaise 256

Day 30 — To Jesus, Eternal Light 257

DECEMBER 258

Day 1 — To Mary, Mother of Advent ... 259

Day 2 — To Jesus, Good Shepherd 259

Day 3 — To the Holy Spirit, Spirit of Joy 260

Day 4 — In Honor of St. Nicholas 260

Day 5 — To St. John Bosco 261

Day 6 — To Divine Mercy................... 262

Day 7 — To St. Clare of Assisi............ 262

Day 8 — To the Holy Spirit................. 263

Day 9 — To St. Lucy........................... 263

Day 10 — To St. Teresa of Avila 264

Day 11 — To Saint Joseph, Protector of Families... 264

Day 12 — To Mary, Seat of Wisdom.... 266

Day 13 — To St. Gabriel the Archangel 267

Day 14 — To the Eucharistic Lord 268

Day 15 — To St. John the Apostle....... 268

Day 16 — To St. Benedict................... 269

Day 17 — To Divine Hope................... 269

Day 18 — To St. Anthony of Padua 270

Day 19 — Daily Prayer to St. Nicholas 271

Day 20 — Prayer to the Sacred Heart of Jesus 273

Day 21 — To St. Raphael the Archangel 274

Day 22 — To the Holy Spirit, Giver of New Beginnings 274

Day 23 — To St. Faustina 275

Day 24 — To Jesus, Light of the Nations 275

Day 25 — To the Infant Jesus............. 276

Day 26 — To Saint Joseph the Worker 277

Day 27 — To Holy Spirit , giver of spiritual gifts and guidance. 278

Day 28 — To the Holy Family............. 279

Day 29 — To St. Bridget of Sweden 279

Day 30 — To Heavenly Father, Divine Healer 280

Day 31 — To Jesus, My Strength and My Promise 280

A Thanksgiving Prayer at Year's End 282

Daily Affirmation — Health, Wealth, Love, and Success... 283

Prayer for Courage....................................... 283

Prayer for the Gifts of the Holy Spirit............ 284

Prayer for the Fruits of the Holy Spirit 285

Prayer Before Work 286

Infant Jesus of Prague Novena Prayer 288

Prayer to the Holy Family 289

Chaplet of Divine Mercy 291

The Apostles' Creed 293

The Lord's Prayer 294

Rosary: How to Pray the Rosary 295

Joyful Mysteries — Monday & Saturday 296

Sorrowful Mysteries — Tuesday & Friday 298

Glorious Mysteries — Wednesday & Sunday 301

Luminous Mysteries — Thursday 304

Hail Holy Queen... 306

Litany of the Blessed Virgin Mary (Litany of Loreto) 308

Saints 312

Find Prayer: 315

www.ingramcontent.com/pod-product-compliance
Lightning Source LLC
Chambersburg PA
CBHW032147080426
42735CB00008B/619